TWAYNE'S WORLD AUTHORS SERIES
A Survey of the World's Literature

RUSSIA

Charles Moser

EDITOR

Alexander Ostrovsky

TWAS 611

Alexander Ostrovsky
Courtesy of the Bakhrushin Theater Museum, Moscow

ALEXANDER OSTROVSKY

By Marjorie L. Hoover

TWAYNE PUBLISHERS

A DIVISION OF G. K. HALL & CO., BOSTON

Library of Congress Cataloging in Publication Data

Hoover, Marjorie L.
Alexander Ostrovsky.

(Twayne's world authors series ; TWAS 611 : Russia)
Bibliography: p. 146–52
Includes index.
1. Ostrovskii, Aleksandr Nikolaevich,
1823-1886—Criticism and interpretation.
PG3337.08Z652   891.72'3   80-19152
ISBN 0-8057-6453-4

"возвращайтесь
вспять
к слоновой кости,
к мамонту,
к Островскому
назад."

Маяковский

Contents

About the Author

Born in New York City, Marjorie Hoover received degrees in the U.S. and Germany, and studied also in France and the U.S.S.R. As Professor of German and Russian at Oberlin College, she published textbook editions of Franz Kafka and Tankred Dorst, as well as translations of Heinrich Böll and Nikolai Erdman. Her articles deal with twentieth century literature and theater in both German and Russian. Her book, *Meyerhold: The Art of Conscious Theater,* was nominated for a National Book Award in 1975.

Preface

When asked who was the greatest French poet, André Gide is said to have replied, "Alas, Victor Hugo." If asked, "Who is our greatest dramatist?" a Russian would undoubtedly name Alexander Ostrovsky, and perhaps with the same sigh. At least it was customary to think thus when D. S. Mirsky wrote his classic *History of Russian Literature* in 1925. However, that was before the past half-century's steadily increasing interest in Ostrovsky.

Two great critics who surveyed the first ten years of Ostrovsky's plays upon their publication in a two-volume edition in 1859 made them seem his characteristic achievement in the eyes of succeeding generations. One of them—Nikolay Chernyshevsky—saw in their innovatively Realistic picture of the world of Moscow small business a politically progressive protest against that world. The other—Nikolay Dobrolyubov—also considered them a protest against "the dark kingdom" of that petty bourgeois world, with its domestic tyranny. When another critic of the time, Dmitry Pisarev, tried to modify the notion of conscious protest in Ostrovsky's greatest play, *The Storm* (1860), he was largely ignored. Likewise, the poet and critic Apollon Grigorev's appreciation of the lyric and tragic strains in the same play passed unheeded. Tolstoy compared another of Ostrovsky's comedies of the same period to Alexander Griboedov's great classic *Woe from Wit* for its depiction of government circles, but only in a personal letter.[1] Thus the stereotype of Ostrovsky as bard of the narrow Moscow merchant world prevailed for decades.

No critics of comparable stature appeared in the period after the liberation of the serfs to interpret Ostrovsky's further development. Instead, what critics there were reproached him for not repeating his earlier achievement, or told him that the age in which he had made his reputation was gone. However, as the modern scholar Efim Kholodov puts it, it was not "Ostrovsky's time" which had gone, but "that of his critics."[2] He continued to produce: he wrote historical plays for a time, and even a fairy-tale play in verse. He satirized speculators on the way up, and aristocrats on the way down in capitalist society. He depicted women without viable means of support seeking security, and actresses leading the life of the theater. Avoiding the mere successions of scenes characteristic of his early Realistic style, he wrote carefully structured plays, even perpetrating the surprise ending in his late work. He no longer wrote quaint dialogue, but the colloquial language of society.

Interest in the larger view of Ostrovsky's work was stimulated at the centennial of his birth in 1923, in part by Anatoly Lunacharsky's slogan "Back to Ostrovsky." The early Soviet years engendered not only radical productions of his plays, but also scholarly activity, including the publication of his diaries and letters, and eventually the issuance of the first full edition of his work, including over forty plays, diaries, articles, speeches, and letters.

Ostrovsky's reputation in the West shows something of the same periodicity. After the first obligatory translation by Constance Garnett of *The Storm,* just before the turn of the century, interest in his work intensified in the 1920s with the translations of George Rapall Noyes, that American pioneer in the field of Russian literature. The situation improved after World War II with new translations—especially those by David Magarshack—and the inclusion of Ostrovsky's plays in anthologies. However, later Western interest—attested by the translations of Eugene Bristow—cannot match the steadily increasing attention Ostrovsky has received in the USSR. Spurred by the one-hundred-fiftieth anniversary of his birth in 1973, it has led to a still fuller edition of his work, now in process of publication.

This study seeks first to make Ostrovsky better known in the English-speaking world; second, to expand the confining view of him as the exponent of "the dark kingdom" and its domestic tyranny alone; and finally, to show him rather as a great interpreter of amazing women. What increment of profit might then come to theater lovers, if this revised image should lead to imaginative interpretation of Ostrovsky's work on stage.

MARJORIE L. HOOVER

Chronology

1823   March 31: Alexander Nikolaevich Ostrovsky born in Moscow, son of a municipal court official.

1840   Graduates from the gymnasium with *magna cum laude* in most subjects; enters Moscow University as a law student.

1843   Leaves the university to become clerk of municipal court. Finishes his first story.

1847   February 14: reads the short play *A Scene of Family Bliss* at Professor Stepan Shevyrev's; publishes it, his first complete work in print, March 14 in the *Moscow Municipal Bulletin.* Father buys a country place at Shchelykovo, Kostroma province.

1849   Takes Agafya Ivanovna (last name unknown) as his common-law wife; is therefore cut off by his father. Completes his first full-length play, *A Family Affair.*

1850   Mikhail Pogodin, editor of the *Muscovite,* in No. 6 (March) of which *A Family Affair* appeared, asks that Ostrovsky recruit a "young editorial board" for the magazine. Nicholas I, confirming the censor's prohibition of *A Family Affair* for the stage, orders police surveillance of "the literary man Ostrovsky."

1851   Loses civil service post because of police surveillance.

1853   February 14: first play to be staged, *Stay in Your Own Lane,* enjoys great success at the Maly Theater, Moscow. A second play, *The Poor Bride,* reaches the stage that year, and a third, *Poverty's No Vice,* is in rehearsal by December.

1856   Begins publishing in Nikolay Nekrasov and Ivan Panaev's magazine *The Contemporary,* in which until its closure by the government (1866) most of Ostrovsky's plays of the next decade appear.

1856–   Makes an expedition to the sources of the Volga for the
1857   Marine Ministry, keeping a diary of findings.

1858   Yielding to the censor's demand for a moral ending, gets *A Family Affair* on stage at last. Publishes first collected edition of works in two volumes with G. A. Kushelev-Bezborodko, dated 1859.

1859   Nikolay Dobrolyubov's famous article on the first ten years of Ostrovsky's career, "The Dark Kingdom," appears. *The Storm* produced at the Maly and Alexandrinsky.

1860   *The Storm* receives the Uvarov Prize, and is reviewed in Dobrolyubov's second article, "A Ray of Light in the Dark Kingdom."

1861   The playreading committee of the Imperial theaters reverses its rejection of the third part of the Balzaminov trilogy as a result of a letter from Ostrovsky and widespread protest.

1862   Frustrated by rejections and prohibitions, and also following the fashion, Ostrovsky turns for several years to writing history plays. Travels abroad to the major cities of Europe.

1863   Receives the Uvarov Prize for *Sin and Sorrow Are Common to All*.

1865   *Dream on the Volga* staged at the Mariinsky and the Bolshoi Theaters. November 14: founds the Actors' Club.

1867   Peter Tschaikovsky writes opera of *Dream on the Volga*. Agafya Ivanovna dies. With his brother Mikhail buys Shchelykovo from their stepmother.

1868   With *The Diary of a Scoundrel* begins publishing in *Fatherland Notes*, now acquired by Nekrasov and Mikhail Saltykov-Shchedrin, in which twenty-one of his plays will appear before government closure of the magazine (1884).

1869   Marries the actress Maria Vasileva (real name Bakhmeteva) in church.

1870   Finishes "Memorandum on a Copyright for Dramatists." Initiates Association of Russian Playwrights and Opera Composers.

1872   Twenty-fifth anniversary of his career in the theater celebrated; his request for a pension refused by the ministry.

1873   Tschaikovsky writes music for *The Snow Maiden*, which opens at the Bolshoi.

1876   Nikolay Solovev stays at Shchelykovo to collaborate on two plays, the second of which, *The Marriage of Belugin*, signed by both collaborators, scores a great success the next year.

1881   Uncensored version of *A Family Affair* finally staged by the Pushkin Theater of Anna Brenko, Moscow.

1881–   Works on the Imperial commission examining the theater
1882   situation, submitting "A Memorandum on the Situation of Dramatic Art at the Present Time," and one "On Theater Schools."

Chronology

1882 Nikolai Rimsky-Korsakov's opera *The Snow Maiden* opens at the Mariinsky. Celebrates thirty-fifth anniversary of career in the theater. Request for a government pension rejected.

1884 Granted an audience and a pension of 3,000 rubles annually by Alexander III.

1885 *Not of This World* opens at the Maly and Alexandrinsky. Suffers an attack of angina pectoris.

1886 Appointed director of repertory for the Moscow Imperial theaters. Works on translation of Shakespeare's *Antony and Cleopatra*. Suffers violent attack of angina pectoris while in St. Petersburg to render report on Moscow theaters. Returning to Shchelykovo to rest, continues to work on *Antony and Cleopatra*, and an article on the actor's art. June 2: dies of a fatal attack of angina pectoris.

CHAPTER 1

Man of the Theater

I *All Beginnings Are Hard*

THE mention of a playwright's name usually brings to mind his best-known heroes: Shakespeare, and one thinks of Hamlet, or Romeo and Juliet; Racine, and one pictures Andromaque or Phèdre; Goethe, and one sees Faust and Mephistopheles; Chekhov, and one hears Lopakhin reasoning with Ranevskaya. Such immediate impressions distort the whole work of no great dramatist so drastically as does the all too frequent identification of Ostrovsky with the figures of his early plays, taken from the middle-class business world into which he himself was born in Moscow on March 31, 1823.

Just as his work soon moves beyond the Moscow business world of the early plays, so he himself soon leaves behind his association with it. His father, Nikolay, who came from the provincial city of Kostroma, owed his love of books to his early seminary training for the priesthood. Ostrovsky's grandfather, himself a priest, had sent Nikolay to Moscow to the Theological Academy; he himself later came to the metropolis to become a monk in the Donskoy Monastery, where his grandson Alexander used to visit him until his death in 1843.

Nikolay Ostrovsky exemplified that ferment of social change noticeable everywhere in Europe even in the period of so-called reaction following the Napoleonic Wars. Instead of entering the priesthood, he took a post in the judiciary branch of the civil service, and then represented business interests in civil suits. He prospered so markedly that upon the death of Alexander's mother when the boy was eight—she too had come from church circles—Nikolay took as his second wife a baroness of Swedish descent. Thanks to his second wife's coat of arms, the father was able to enter the whole family in the Moscow register of nobility.

In the formal sense Alexander was thus a nobleman, though

15

actually he stemmed from the business world. His father, who eventually owned a couple of houses in the Zamoskvoreche (Beyond the Moscow River) district of Moscow and could afford to marry the Baroness Emilia von Tessin, was also in a position to give his nine children a good education. Alexander was at first tutored in French and German at home; he then went to a Moscow gymnasium, graduating with grades good enough to admit him without further examination to the university. His father, though, would not allow his eldest son to choose the liberal arts curriculum he wished to take, but required him to study law. Little as Alexander had recorded of his early youth, still, almost half a century later, when requested to supply a few lines to accompany a portrait published in an album by a St. Petersburg photographer, he specifically recalled this parental interference with his inclination.[1]

Yet Alexander owed his love for literature in part to his father's extensive library, in which he had read widely. He was, further, by then incurably addicted to the theater, where he had been taken since childhood, and where he had spent all his free time in high school. His heroes were the actors of the Moscow Maly Theater, still those of Gogol's time: the tragedian Pavel Mochalov, perhaps greatest as Hamlet; and the comedian Mikhail Shchepkin, most famous as the mayor in Gogol's *The Inspector General*.

Bowing to his father's wish, however, that he enter the law and business, Alexander matriculated in the law faculty and with characteristic family diligence passed the first-year exams in the spring of 1841. But two of his closest professors were in different fields: his professor of literature, Stepan Shevyrev, at whose house he read his first play; and his professor of history, Mikhail Pogodin, who published Ostrovsky's first full-length play in his magazine *Moskvityanin* (The Muscovite).

Though Alexander was, it seems, basically shy and lonely, he moved constantly in a crowd of merry companions. Evgeny Edelson, Terty Filippov, and Apollon Grigorev accompanied him in serious discussions at cafés, evenings at the theater, and nights in taverns. He must have begun to lead such a Bohemian life while at the university, since he excused himself as sick from his second-year law exams in the spring of 1842. He then repeated the second year, and when he did take the examinations in 1843 he received an unsatisfactory grade in the history of Roman law. Without waiting to be dropped from the university, he himself requested his dismissal and was granted his request on May 22, 1843. Thereupon his father obtained a place for him as clerk in a Moscow civil court which encouraged the conciliatory settlement of civil disputes without resort to due process.[2] While working in this capacity, the young man became acquainted with the cheating and corruption common in the business world, if he had not already done so through the cases with which his father dealt.

The young clerk of court must hardly have slept at all during this period. Besides working at his daytime job and spending nights with his friends, he completed an early story, "Kak kvartal'nyi nadziratel' puskalsia v plias" (How the Police Precinct Captain Went on a Binge). This early prose piece about a downtrodden official who, paycheck and all, is taken in hand by a widow with many children unmistakably derives from Gogol's masterpiece "The Overcoat." Ostrovsky partly reused this early work in the story "Zapiski zamoskvoretskogo zhitelia" (Notes of a Beyond-the-River Resident), which he published in the *Moskovsky gorodskoy listok* (Moscow Town Bulletin) in 1847.

Ostrovsky's first published story is both derivative and innovative. It shows itself a firstling by its use of a worn device: the narrator pretends to have found a manuscript. "This manuscript," he says, "throws light on a country as yet never described, . . . on the way of life of its inhabitants, their language, customs, manners, level of education—all this has been obscured in the murk of the unknown."[3] The new land revealed in the story is Ostrovsky's home area of Moscow. His pretense at sociological description is neither new nor peculiarly his own; rather it belongs to the genre of the "physiological sketch," which in the 1830s became the literary fashion, with Dickens's *Sketches by Boz;* Balzac's "studies," as he called the groupings of his novels in "Scenes of Provincial Life," and "Scenes of Parisian Life"; or Gogol's picture of St. Petersburg life reflected in a street, "Nevsky Prospect." If by the end of the 1840s Ostrovsky's documentary pose was thus not new, the territory he set out to discover across the river was, though, indeed a newfound land all his own.

While Ostrovsky was breaking into print, his father had secured his transfer to a post in Commercial Court. Nikolay Ostrovsky also bought a country place—Shchelykovo in Kostroma province—the family's only basis for their rank as nobility. It was there in 1848 that Alexander spent his first summer away from Moscow. Perhaps the father hoped the sojourn would distract his twenty-five-year-old son from an attachment he had formed for a girl not his social equal.

Unlike others of his age, however, Alexander continued his relationship with the young woman, Agafya Ivanovna, and, when he stayed behind in Moscow the following summer, even moved her into his father's house. Thereupon his father cut him off from further financial support.

In the meantime, since 1847, Ostrovsky had been acquiring a literary name and fame. His first one-act play, *Kartina semeinogo schast'ia* (A Scene of Family Bliss), was publicly hailed when he read it on February 14, 1847, at Professor Shevyrev's. After the reading the professor jumped to his feet and proclaimed to those present that Ostrovsky was "a new hope for the drama in Russian literature."[4] Among those present was the critic of the *Moskovsky gorodskoy listok*, Apollon Grigorev, whom Ostrovsky at that time barely knew. Despite Shevyrev's encouragement, Ostrovsky could not bring himself to sign his play when it appeared in the same issue of the *Listok* in which Grigorev remarked on it in his weekly column. The editors paid Ostrovsky forty rubles, his first literary fee. This reading and publication were two of the four events which—in the last year of his life—he found worth remarking in the information he submitted for Mikhail Semevsky's album of autobiographical entries from famous people.

Still, if Ostrovsky's calling as a dramatist was twice confirmed in 1847, that year also witnessed the first of many rebuffs to recognition of his plays: the censor forbade the staging of *A Scene of Family Bliss*. Perhaps the wonder is not that throughout his life Ostrovsky had constantly to overcome difficulties with the censor, but that he got so many plays on stage at all. Such great predecessors as Alexander Griboedov and Pushkin each created one major work for the theater without seeing it produced in their lifetime, which explains in part why neither became a prolific playwright: who knowingly writes plays for the drawer! The censor's greater hesitation to pass a play for production than for publication is obviously due to the larger public impact which the theater has had on an assembly since its origins in ritual and festival, an impression of more consequence than that made on a single reader by the printed page.

Pogodin was the host of Ostrovsky's next triumphant reading, when Ostrovsky and the actor Prov Sadovsky read divided roles of *Svoi liudi sochtemsia* (A Family Affair), the dramatist's first full-length play, on December 3, 1849. Gogol and the great Gogolian actor Shchepkin were present, and Gogol is said to have passed an approving note to the young author, anointing, as it were, the young dramatist as his successor; though no such note has been found, still its legend persists.[5] Hoping *A Family Affair* would help bring new life to his magazine, Pogodin published it in *Moskvityanin* for March 1850.

Publication, however, brought Ostrovsky's play no closer to production, for the playwright had emerged upon the literary scene at an unfavorable moment. In 1848 revolutions in France and Germany had further shaken the confidence of the already distrustful emperor Nicholas I, and many intellectuals—including Fedor Dostoevsky—were arrested in the spring of 1849. Still, Pogodin persuaded Moscow officials in responsible censorship positions—Professor V. N. Leshkov, General Vladimir Nazimov, and Count Arseny Zakrevsky—to hear Ostrovsky read *A Family Affair*. After these official readings, which sufficed to procure permission to publish, Ostrovsky at first held his play back, as if fearing to put it forward at an unfavorable time. Later, when he petitioned Count Zakrevsky, the governor general, for permission to stage it, he apparently overestimated the importance of the count's favorable reaction at the reading. True-blue official that he was, Zakrevsky passed on the request to his St. Petersburg superior, Court Minister Prince P. M. Volkonsky, who, in turn, submitted it to a committee, which ruled first in favor of and then against the play's production, so that the final decision was left to His Imperial Majesty himself. Nicholas I personally confirmed the committee's second judgment in a pencil scrawl. To be sure, he wrote without commas, so that his comment could be read as more severe than it was perhaps meant to be: "Absolutely right, it shouldn't have been published, prohibit its production in any case. . . ." Or did the phrase "in any case" belong with the final clause? "In any case inform Prince Volkonsky of this."[6]

In any case, the decision not only stopped the staging of *A Family Affair,* it also kept it from being discussed in the press: it was not mentioned, much less reviewed, throughout the year of its publication. Not until twelve years after its appearance—in the emancipation year of 1861—was it finally allowed on stage, and it was produced then only after Ostrovsky had agreed to change the ending so as to suggest the edifying moral that crime does not pay.

The moral and educational mission of the theater was taken for granted in nineteenth-century Russia as much by the authorities as by the playwrights themselves. Thus Nicholas and Ostrovsky agreed that the theater should have a moral effect, and the young man so declared in response to the emperor's inquiry. For Nicholas also wrote on the censorship committee report: "Who is Ostrovsky, author of *A Family Affair?*", a query which set off a chain reaction back down through all echelons. Since the report of Ostrovsky's superior at Commercial Court was altogether favorable, the police investigator could tell Count Zakrevsky nothing: "He is a person of good conduct and unblemished life, but it is impossible to make positive conclusions about his way of thinking."[7] This sufficed for Nicholas to order Ostrovsky placed under secret surveillance, about which the victim learned at once when General Nazimov, responsible for carrying out the order, summoned him to protest his own personal good will. Ostrovsky, in turn, responded to the interview with Nazimov by defining in writing his view of the dramatist's vocation. Citing the biblical notion that we must each use our God-given talent, and that his was for writing comedies, he called "comedy the best form for the attainment of moral goals."[8] Ostrovsky, however, depicted the world as far removed from perfect morality, whereas Nicholas demanded that it be shown rather as morally perfect. Unfortunately the dramatist could have no effect—moral or otherwise—upon the public as long as the emperor prevented his play from reaching any audience at all.

Ostrovsky then tried other means of reaching an audience. At first the young writer found audiences at literary readings in professorial circles, then at aristocratic houses. One literary hostess, for example, heard *A Family Affair* at Pogodin's and invited the author to her Saturday "at homes." All the next winter the play was read at such occasions, not always by Ostrovsky alone and not in Moscow alone. The young literary lion of aristocratic salons also seems to have dressed the part. Tall, with reddish hair and blue-gray eyes, he affected plaid trousers with a frock coat, and carried a cane. However, he soon gave up such readings in favor of his true calling as a professional dramatist.

His first professional steps were fraught with disillusionment. In March 1850 Pogodin persuaded him to become the editor of the *Moskvityanin,* a conservative, Slavophile organ which generally adopted a positive view of the Russian people. Pogodin hoped Ostrovsky could revitalize the magazine by bringing in his friends Edelson, Filippov, and Grigorev to form a "young editorial board." In the next few months, though, Ostrovsky and the new board which had thought it would be responsible to Ostrovsky were disturbed to find that Pogodin still exercised final authority. Ostrovsky was naturally the most hindered not only in editorial, but also in financial matters, as he had to persuade Pogodin to pay for the manuscripts he accepted, and even to obtain payment for his own work. His many letters to Pogodin over the next three years were mostly filled with requests for money. Almost a year after assuming editorship, still with no firm contract, he wrote to Pogodin on February 25, 1851: "Write me whether you can give me fifty rubles in silver per month simply for my collaboration. I, for my part, obligate myself to contribute articles for this amount in the course of the year, and I retain the right also to contribute articles to other publications."9

Beside lack of authority and a clear contract, Ostrovsky had other difficulties at the *Moskvityanin*. He fell short of his plan to contribute criticism, for he wrote only two reviews, neither of which was notable for critical gifts. One—a review of a story by Evgenya Tur—shows him groping for critical principles; the other—a review of a story by his friend Alexey Pisemsky, *The Simpleton*—is no more than a plot summary, which was the more unnecessary as *The Simpleton* had earlier appeared in the *Moskvityanin*. But if he published little criticism, he did publish two further plays of his own in the magazine: *Bednaia nevesta* (The Poor Bride, 1852) and *Ne v svoi sani ne sadis'* (Stay in Your Own Lane, 1853). Even then he had difficulty in obtaining payment for them. No wonder his initial enthusiasm for the magazine diminished.

The successful production of *Stay in Your Own Lane* a few months before its publication was a true turning point in Ostrovsky's life, and he recorded the date of this first premiere of a play of his on stage—January 14, 1853, at the Maly Theater in Moscow—as one of four memorable fourteenths of the month in Semevsky's album. This play favorably depicts the middle-class business world which had been shown so unfavorably in *A Family Affair*. Does this turnabout represent compromise on Ostrovsky's part with his principles for the sake of success? Or had the *Moskvityanin*'s Slavophilism converted him to love of the Russian people? Ostrovsky himself avowed in a letter to Pogodin of September 30, 1853: "My bent is beginning to change; my view of life in my first play seems to me youthful and too harsh. Let my fellow Russian be glad rather than sad at seeing himself on stage."10

Stage success came threefold to Ostrovsky in 1853. The success of his play of the new "bent" at the Imperial theaters of both Moscow and St. Petersburg swept *The Poor Bride* as well to production at the same theaters; and by December a third play, *Bednost' ne porok* (Poverty Is No Vice), was in rehearsal at the Maly. His success became, however, a necessity for him, too. Ostrovsky had lost his job in Commercial Court by January 1851 because of the police surveillance his first play had engendered. And his first production came too late to change his father's mind, for he died at Shchelykovo too early in 1853 to learn of it, leaving his supposedly dissolute son almost without inheritance. Thus, Ostrovsky was soon compelled to earn his living as a playwright.

II   *The Established Playwright*

Though from now on Ostrovsky may be considered a playwright of repute, a new obstacle joined the old ones of censorship and finances: Pavel Fedorov, who was from 1854 to 1879 director of repertory at the St. Petersburg Imperial theaters, that is, the person responsible for selecting the plays to be produced by the theaters of the tsarist monopoly. Ostrovsky had endlessly to beg the intervention with Fedorov of his two advocates in St. Petersburg: his younger brother Mikhail, who eventually rose to be senator and a court minister of influence; and the actor Fedor Burdin, who proved always a staunch friend to Ostrovsky.

Far from offering any obstacles, the critics initially hailed Ostrovsky. Critical controversy arose later, and over a play which the author explicitly cited as an example of his new "bent," meant to please: *Bednost' ne porok* (Poverty Is No Vice). That Ostrovsky saw good in its hero—Lyubim Tortsov, the wronged brother of a wealthy business man—raised a storm of discussion because Lyubim is a drunkard. The critics professed even greater shock when in his next play, *Ne tak zhivi, kak khochetsia* (Don't Live as You Like, 1854), he took as his heroine a woman who also drank excessively.

Rising above prudish objection, the poet and critic Apollon Grigorev, who had early remarked Ostrovsky's first one-act play,[11] now touted the tragic dignity of Lyubim "with his pure Russian soul."[12] Grigorev further sensed the poetry and lyric atmosphere in Ostrovsky's discovery of another new world in the provincial Volga town of the dramatist's perhaps greatest play *Groza* (The Storm, 1860). Yet both Ostrovsky's reception at the time and his image henceforth—perhaps even his own notion of his work—were definitively shaped by two other critics of sociopolitical bent. Nikolay Chernyshevsky saw in Ostrovsky's early plays a telling exposure of corruption and the advocacy of a new social order, while Nikolay Dobrolyubov even with the title of his survey of the playwright's first ten years, "Temnoe tsarstvo" (The Dark Kingdom), viewed the early plays as castigating oppression. Dobrolyubov termed the abuse of authority exposed there *samodurstvo* in his first article of 1859, which he followed with a second in the same magazine, the *Sovremennik* (The Contemporary), upon the appearance of *The Storm* the year after. The second article, "Luch sveta v temnom tsarstve" (A Ray of Light in the Dark Kingdom), hailed Katherine's suicide in the play as a protest against *samodurstvo* and hence "a ray of light" in the dark world of oppression.

The Storm proves Ostrovsky to be the Columbus of more than the Moscow Beyond-the-River district. Perhaps because he had been born and bred in the city, he appreciated the landscapes of Russia more deeply, and conveyed that appreciation to audiences in several of his plays. For instance, in an early diary he jotted down impressions of a trip to Nizhny Novgorod in 1845 in single words, though the words swell to phrases as he viewed the countryside with fresh eyes: "I go out to the shore of the river—and the Volga opens out, sand and the low bank, as far as the eye reaches, cities, villages, lakes."[13] On his first trip to Shchelykovo in 1848 he experienced the forest for the first time. The new estate seen in reality delights him as much more, he writes, "as nature is better than one dreams it."[14] The summers spent at Shchelykovo thereafter and the repeated trips there—especially after he and his brother purchased the estate from their stepmother in 1867—reinforced the depictions of the Volga, the forest and provincial life which are as characteristic of some Ostrovsky plays as is in others that of the Moscow Beyond-the-River district.

In 1856 Ostrovsky obtained a much more fundamental acquaintance with the Volga than the summer traveler's when he undertook a trip to its sources for the Marine Ministry. In order to be appointed for the study trip, he had to be relieved of the police surveillance ordered by Nicholas I, which proved easy enough in the new reign of Alexander II. The ministry commissioned studies of several rivers so as to learn how much river navigation and fishing prepared recruits from the river regions to be better sailors in the Imperial navy. Doubtless one reason for appointing writers to undertake these missions was a wish to improve the quality of the maritime journal in which their reports were published. Ostrovsky found the once important shipping and fishing industries of the

Volga to have decayed almost to the point of disappearance, and so reported in the only article he published in fulfillment of his mission.[15]

Ostrovsky's trip to the sources of the Volga may not have been very useful for the ministry, but it was highly rewarding for the playwright's own work. True, when he fractured his leg in July 1856 he could not work at all for several weeks. But after the leg had healed in 1857 he insisted on returning to the Volga and completing his task, which proved its value for him. Certainly, in addition to talks with people from all walks of life in the river towns, he derived from the study an unexpected treasure: a rich knowledge of popular and provincial speech, examples of which he collected on file cards. Maintained over a lifetime, the file at Ostrovsky's death amounted to 1,040 cards. His brother gave them to the Academy of Sciences, which used them in compiling the Academy dictionary. Ostrovsky had noted phonetic, grammatical, and semantic phenomena with the interest and sophistication of the trained philologist.[16]

Aside from popular language, Volga life also penetrated Ostrovsky's plays, some half-dozen of which are set on or near the river. Ostrovsky intended to write still others, but never finished the series he planned, to be called "Nights on the Volga." One such river play with a contemporary subject, *The Storm*, is set in the imaginary town of Kalinov on the Volga, while another, *Bespridannitsa* (Fiancée without Fortune, 1878), is also set in an imaginary river town, Brakhimov. *Son na Volge* (Dream on the Volga, 1865), a historical play, also belongs to the projected Volga series.

Other trips of Ostrovsky's are reflected in diaries and letters, but none had the impact of the Volga study trip on the plays. In 1860, for example, Ostrovsky accompanied the actor Alexander Martynov on a triumphal tour to the South in the interests of the latter's health. Martynov played his roles—including several in Ostrovsky's plays—as if he were not fatally ill of tuberculosis. When he died on the trip, the writer brought his body back to St. Petersburg.

In 1862 Ostrovsky made the grand tour of Europe, also in the company of theater friends from St. Petersburg: Makar Shishko, a creator of special effects, and the actor Ivan Gorbunov. The playwright's diaries and letters about the trip resemble the usual tourist impressions. None of the three could speak the languages of the places visited (Berlin, Paris, London, and the principal Italian cities) though they tried to penetrate beneath the surface by going to the theater—about which Ostrovsky makes quite professional observations—and visiting friends in exile. No written record exists of their conversations with Russians abroad—for example, with Alexander Herzen in London—doubtless for political reasons. Ostrovsky showed himself a companionable person throughout his life. Of his family, he clearly felt closest to his brother Mikhail, though he had strong ties also to his younger half-brother Peter. Several friends made at school and university later participated in the literary circle at Professor Shevyrev's. The closest of these— Boris Almazov, Evgeny Edelson, and Terty Filippov—also joined the *Moskvityanin* editorial board, with which Pisemsky, another university friend, collaborated from afar. When the task of saving *Moskvityanin* proved beyond their powers, the friends moved on to new associations. By 1856 Ostrovsky would be photographed with other creators of the new Realism—Ivan Goncharov, Leo Tolstoy, Ivan Turgenev, and Dmitry Grigorovich—in a famous group picture at the *Sovremennik.*

Ostrovsky's loyalty to the editors of the *Sovremennik,* Nikolay Nekrasov and Ivan Panaev, carried over after its closure by the government in 1866 to the magazine which Nekrasov in partnership with Mikhail Saltykov-Shchedrin began editing in January 1868, *Otechestvyennye zapiski* (Fatherland Notes). Ostrovsky also enjoyed the literary friendship of Fedor Dostoevsky, editor of *Vremya* (Time), in which he published some of his works.

However, Ostrovsky's warmest associations and lifelong friendships—even his loves, at least after the first—belong to the theater, in which after 1853 he came more and more to live day and night. In *Stay in Your Own Lane,* which launched Ostrovsky in the theater, the lead was played by Lyubov Kositskaya, who later created the role of Katherine in *The Storm.* He fell in love with Kositskaya, though she then left him for another. Ostrovsky, incidentally, always conceived plays with a particular actor or actress in mind, as he wrote late in life to the actress Maria Savina, for whom he created the role of Larisa in *Fiancée without Fortune:* "I have written all my best works for some great talent, and under the influence of that talent."[17]

No genius, and not even very talented, was the young actress Maria Vasileva (stage name; real name Bakhmeteva), by whom Ostrovsky had had two children even before Agafya Ivanovna's death in 1867 and whom he finally married in 1869. Surely not so much love as concern for his six children and his characteristic constancy enabled Ostrovsky from then on to endure Vasileva's quite-domineering conduct of their life. She brought the theater even to Shchelykovo with amateur theatricals, in which her husband took no part; all he wanted there was quiet to continue his work. In view of his absorption with the theater, it is not surprising that a well-known group picture of 1863 no longer shows Ostrovsky among literary associates at the *Sovremennik*, but reading to a group of actors at the theater: Burdin, Gorbunov, Kositskaya. Of course, the playwright's theater friendships were not free of difficulties. The great actor Prov Sadovsky, who gave an outstanding performance as the drunken blacksheep brother in *Poverty's No Vice*, was himself given to the bottle; once, to the indignation of his friend the playwright, he actually fell asleep on stage in *Dream on the Volga* (the Russian title, *Son na Volge*, means literally "sleep on the Volga").

Ostrovsky's most loyal theater friend was perhaps Fedor Burdin, who repeatedly fought for the acceptance of the dramatist's plays by the St. Petersburg playreading committee. Though he was a less than gifted actor, Ostrovsky—in return for his intercession with the committee—repeatedly gave him important roles. When the playwright directed *The Storm*, he tried to mitigate his friend's excesses, yet Pisemsky said that, in the role of the narrow-minded tyrant Dikoy, Burdin "so threw himself around, roared so loud . . . that he almost swallowed the chandeliers."[18]

After 1870 Ostrovsky felt that his personal life was over, and that in going from Moscow to Shchelykovo he merely exchanged one work desk for another. His family required ever more money, and his actor friends pleaded for ever more "benefits"—plays from which, with the author's consent, a single actor received the whole box-office take for a designated performance. Besides, large sums went for the entertainment of friends at Shchelykovo: thus provisions were hauled in quantity from the best Moscow stores each spring for the many house guests who for weeks at a time enjoyed the freedom of living there as they pleased. From his youth on, Ostrovsky still went his own way amid a constant crowd of friends.

III *Ostrovsky and Officialdom*

In return for his devotion to the theater Ostrovsky enjoyed both recognition and rejection. Thus he twice won the officially sponsored Uvarov Prize for drama, perhaps the greatest honor officialdom could accord him: in 1860 for *The Storm*, and in 1863 for *Grekh da beda na kogo ne zhivet* (Sin and Sorrow Are Common to All). But prohibition accompanied the award when the staging of *The Storm* was forbidden in Odessa because of its treatment of adultery, and this at a time when Ostrovsky and Martynov were honored at a banquet there on their tour of 1860. In the year of the second Uvarov Prize the St. Petersburg playreading committee rejected Part III of the Balzaminov trilogy as farce too low for the Imperial theaters, whereupon Ostrovsky threatened to quit writing for the stage. Again the fate of the historical play, entitled with the hero's name *Kozma Zakharich Minin, Sukhoruk*, examplifies the same back and forth of reward and rejection: upon its publication in the *Sovremennik* in 1862 it so pleased the emperor Alexander II that he sent the author a ring worth 500 rubles, and oral commendation, but the play was then prohibited for the stage in 1863.

Reward and rebuke continued in close succession for some time. In 1866 Ostrovsky hoped for the customary jubilee in celebration of his twenty years of work. When no such occasion was organized, he wrote Burdin in September declaring his intent to go on writing, but not for the theater.[19] The rejection that same month of his historical play on the False Dmitry by the playreading committee confirmed his resolve. Yet his despair was moderated by the reversal of the ruling against *Minin*, and its performance, after all, in December 1866.

The anniversary year of 1872, which marked twenty-five years since the publication of *A Family Affair*, also had its ups and downs. On the one hand, the jubilee was celebrated by such organizations as the Moscow Artistic Circle, the St. Petersburg Association of Artists, and the Society of Russian Dramatists and Composers; he was presented with a gold wreath and a citation by the Alexandrinsky Theater company on the first night of *Dmitrii Samozvanets i Vasilii Shuiskii* (The False Dmitry and Vasily Shuisky). On the other hand, the Ministry refused Ostrovsky's application for a pension. Nor was he allowed a pension in 1882, the thirty-fifth anniversary of his first play, by which point he had garnered numerous honors and honorary offices,[20] written some of his best plays, by then collected in a nine-volume edition of his work, had operas composed to his texts,[21] and been chosen with other great writers to appear at the unveiling of the Pushkin Monument in 1880. Only in 1884 was a pension awarded at a gratifying private audience with the emperor Alexander III, but its annual stipend of 3,000 rubles still fell far short of the amount Ostrovsky felt he needed and deserved.

The playwright had ample reason to feel that he deserved better from the Russian government, even aside from his extensive and remarkable contributions to the creative literature of the stage. For instance, for years he had thought and written on the difficulties which hindered the full development of the Russian theater, and sought the explanation of the relative poverty of dramatic literature compared to other genres of that time. Thus in a memorandum of 1863, "Circumstances Hindering the Development of Dramatic Art in Russia," he analyzed three causes for the poverty of the Russian repertory: censorship; the "playreading committee" *(teatral' noliteraturnyi komitet)* instituted by Pavel Fedorov upon his appointment as arbiter of repertory for the Imperial theaters, evidently so as to obscure his responsibility for making the acceptance of plays difficult; and finally, insufficient financial reward to dramatic authors, as well as their near lack of legal rights, including copyright and the right of consent to production.

Censorship, Ostrovsky wrote in his memorandum, causes dramatic authors so to fear the prohibition of their work that they exercise self-censorship before submitting it. As for the playreading committee, Ostrovsky pointed out that its qualified members, such as Alexey Pisemsky, Apollon Maykov, and Alexander Druzhinin, had resigned to be replaced by members not qualified to judge drama, and yet its prohibition of a dramatic work was final. Further, the amount to be paid by the management of the Imperial theaters to opera composers and dramatic authors for their work was set by the guidelines of the outdated Regulation of 1827, which, though without the force of law, still had the effect of fixing maximum fees. Though Ostrovsky prepared notes urging their review both in 1871 and 1881, the guidelines were not revised upward until March 21, 1882. Finally, with a copyright which ran only five years, the dramatic author could neither prevent private entrepreneurs from producing his work without fee nor forbid productions of poor quality. Ostrovsky compared the dramatic author's disfranchisement after expiration of his short-lived copyright with the opera composer's continued right to allow performance of his work only with his consent and upon payment therefore.

Ostrosky's notes and memoranda—including one entitled "Project for Legislation Concerning Dramatic Property" (1869)—went out to various instances. One was published; another was sent to a new director of the Imperial theaters who Ostrovsky hoped might introduce reforms; still another was submitted to a Commission on the Question of Literary and Artistic Property (1871). In revised form Ostrovsky then put them before a later commission appointed by the emperor to review theater legislation, of which, to his delight, Ostrovsky was made a member, serving in St. Petersburg for five months in 1881–82.

To Ostrovsky's great disappointment, however, little came of his proposals to the commission. True, the fees set by the scale of 1827 were raised, but managers were also permitted to negotiate private agreements with authors for fees below the new scale. However, the commission did extend the dramatic author's copyright to fifty years after his death, so that Ostrovsky felt he would leave his children provided for.

When Ostrovsky submitted his memorandum on dramatic property to the commission of 1871, he tried to anticipate possible objections, and among them the argument that even if adequate fees were required of managers, dramatic authors could hardly hope to collect them single-handedly. Ostrovsky therefore undertook a positive initiative to secure payment for authors by organizing them first in an "assembly" *(sobranie)*, of which he called a meeting in 1870, and then in 1874 in the Society of Dramatic Authors and Composers, of which he was then elected president eleven times in succession.

Ostrovsky furthermore believed, as he wrote in his memorandum "On the Situation of the Dramatic Author" (1869), that "author and actor aid one another; the success of one is inseparable from that of the other."[22] So the playwright sought also to improve the actor's lot. Along with the pianist Nikolay Rubinstein, the actor Prov Sadovsky, and the writer and music critic Vladimir Odoevsky, he initiated the founding in 1865 of the Actors' Club *(Artisticheskii kruzhok)*. (He noted the date of its founding—November 14, 1865—as the last of the four crucial fourteenths in Semevsky's album.) In a later memorandum he said that "it took the place of a theater school, gave to the Moscow stage [the son of Prov] Mikhail and [the latter's wife] Olga Sadovsky. At the club audiences first became acquainted with the enormous talent of Pelegea Strepetova."[23] Professional theater people as active members, and laymen as comembers, benefited mutually from the club: the members found in its restaurant and clubrooms a home away from home free of the dissipation of the taverns; the comembers attended performances and concerts. Thus in 1866 Ostrovsky gave a reading at the club from his play *The False Dmitry*, and young actors staged plays in closed performance. At first games of chance provided income; when they were prohibited in 1867 Ostrovsky feared bankruptcy for the club, despite its cultural florescence and current membership of 700. But by autumn of that year the club received permission to charge for tickets to its shows, so that eventually it could support itself in its own field of competence.

Ostrovsky's belief in the interdependence of author and actor caused him to attend not only to the actor's material well-being, but also to his artistic achievement. He often directed actors in his plays and worked with them to improve their performance. He tried to secure the author's right of consent to productions partly for the actor's sake, so as to prevent performances marred by insufficient rehearsal, and hand-me-down costuming and staging. When the discontinuance of acting classes in 1871 transformed the Imperial theater school into exclusively a ballet school, Ostrovsky campaigned in a series of memoranda for the restoration of training for actors: "You can't be born an actor," he argued, "any more than you can be born a violinist."[24] Ostrovsky's pleas for the professional training of actors went unheeded, however, when he submitted them to the commission of 1881–82. Not until he became director of the Moscow Imperial theaters in the last year of his life was training for actors reinstituted.

Some idea of Ostrovsky's standards for actors may be obtained from several of his memoranda advocating theater schools. He required of the actor a native gift of observation by eye and ear, and of memory to recall emotions even from early childhood: "anger, hate, revenge, threat, horror, deep grief, and quiet, serene expressions of well-being, happiness, and gentle tenderness."[25] Such words might have been written by the great director Konstantin Stanislavsky, who made these ideas the core of his "Method" half a century later. But Ostrovsky went on to formulate ideas which were phrased in almost the same words a quarter century after his death by the eminent "techniques director" Vsevolod Meyerhold: "All this rich material stored in the memory . . . still does not make an actor; to be an actor it isn't enough to know, remember, and imagine—one must know how [to express it]."[26] For, Ostrovsky went on, "an actor is a plastic artist; but can one be not only an artist, but even a decent craftsman without having learned the techniques of one's art or craft?"[27] Finally, he presented a detailed curriculum which would suffice for drama schools even today.

When a memorandum of Ostrovsky's on the failure of the Imperial theaters to maintain the quality of the acting company also brought no change, in 1882 he tried to counter the decline within the monopoly by founding a private theater outside it. He obtained a charter and started to raise money for his theater. Shortly thereafter, however, the emperor abrogated the Imperial monopoly altogether, thus frustrating Ostrovsky's effort by allowing private theaters to mushroom.

Only from within, it seemed, could Ostrovsky hope to raise the artistic level of the Imperial theaters. Hence he entered government service as director of repertory for the Moscow Imperial theaters, with his old friend Apollon Maykov as director of administrative and business affairs. In a memorandum of 1885 he said his task would be to improve the quality and exactitude of performance among theater personnel in all their manifold functions.

On the day he took office—January 1, 1886—Ostrovsky delivered to the assembled personnel an inaugural address of but six lines, concluding with the words: "So let us begin to serve great art."[28] That beginning was brief, unhappily, for on June 2, 1886—his work in the bottle-green uniform of officialdom barely started—he suffered a massive attack of angina pectoris, from which he died at Shchelykovo. He was buried in the cemetery of a village (Berezhki) near Shchelykovo, where there is now a museum dedicated to his life and work.

Ostrovsky's efforts on behalf of authors, actors, and the theater as a whole were so farsighted that few were realized in his lifetime. In the end he came to have an overweening sense of his own importance to the Russian theater, reflected in an "Autobiographical Note" written shortly before his death. After criticizing the Imperial theaters for their failure to further dramatic art, he wrote: "Russian dramatic art has only me. I am all: academy, Maecenas, protection. . . . The young actors . . . regard me as children do their father. . . . With me everything will end; without me the actors will disperse like sheep without a shepherd."[29]

However immodest for him to say this, for some forty years Ostrovsky had in fact meant all to the Russian theater. Stanislavsky entitled his autobiography *My Life in Art.* If Ostrovsky had written an autobiography, he should have called it *My Life in the Theater and for the Theater.* In any case, a bronze statue of the seated playwright before the Maly Theater in Moscow has, since 1925, attested to Ostrovsky's importance as Russia's leading classic dramatist.

CHAPTER 2

Early Plays: Two Fronts of Protest

I *Big Business:* A Family Affair

THAT Ostrovsky's first full-length play was banned for the stage
by the censor, and so had to wait ten years for its premiere in
1860, that Emperor Nicholas I had personally scrawled disapproval
of even its publication, must indicate that it threatened public
morality. Indeed, it was based on Ostrovsky's firsthand observation
in the courts: that dishonesty in business pays even if crime does
not. The exposure in a full-length play of moral cynicism among
businessmen grew from his youthful five-finger exercises in
Realism, for which Ostrovsky found precedents in Honoré de
Balzac's *Scènes de la vie privée* (1832) and Charles Dickens's
Sketches by Boz (1836). Ostrovsky's play at first bore the title
Bankrot (Bankruptcy), which was more indicative of its content than
its present title in proverb form: *Svoi liudi—sochtemsia* (It's All in
the Family; We'll Keep it to Ourselves), usually translated as *A
Family Affair* (1849).

A wily businessman, Samson Bolshov, declares himself bankrupt
in order to pay only part of his debts as permissible in case of
bankruptcy. He assigns his assets to his associate Podkhalyuzin,
whom he thinks he can trust because the latter has meantime
become his son-in-law. The younger man, though, has learned his
lesson from the older one all too well. Instead of sharing with his
father-in-law a profit amounting to the difference between the total
amount owed and the partial payment provided the creditors in the
supposed bankruptcy, the son refuses to make even the partial
payment, and so allows his benefactor and father-in-law to go to
debtor's prison. Bolshov's daughter Lipochka has no pity for her
father either, but thinks only of the clothes and carriages she will
have in her new life with Podkhalyuzin, who now owns everything.
To be sure, in order to get the censor's permission to include the

play in the first edition of his collected works in 1858, Ostrovsky altered the conclusion so that Podkhalyuzin receives a summons to appear in court to account for his assets. Thus the possibility of retribution for his wrongdoing is at least hinted at. By 1881, however, thanks to the efforts of Ostrovsky's brother Mikhail, a government minister, the original conclusion was restored, in which the son-in-law, who has bested his father-in-law and preceptor in rascality, addresses the audience: "Look now, we're opening a new store: we beg the favor of your patronage! Send a small child to buy an onion, and we won't short-change him" (Act IV, Sc. 5; I, 152). It is clear that Podkhalyuzin's business will prosper in rascality.

Indeed, Podkhalyuzin's treachery is even worse than it may appear from this brief summary. For the young man has cheated not only his father-in-law, but also the matchmaker Ustinya Naumovna and the scrivener Rispolozhensky, to both of whom he breaks his promise of great reward for their serving his interests rather than Bolshov's. In Lipochka the upstart has found a proper match: despite her Romantic dreams, she has married him because he made the highest money bid for her hand.

For all their callous self-interest, the characters display understandably human motivation. Indeed, their psychology has the rough simplicity of a woodcut, not the exaggeration of caricature usual with Gogol. Of course, *The Inspector General* set a precedent for the young Ostrovsky, who, like Gogol, gives his figures, if not speaking names, then highly allusive ones: the father is Samson Silych [Strongman] Bolshov [Big Shot], and Podkhalyuzin's name resembles the word for "dastardly flatterer."

Like Alexander Griboedov, author of the classic comedy *Woe from Wit*, Ostrovsky has his middle-class heroine schooled in the genteel arts of music, French, and dancing. But while Griboedov's aristocratic Sophie has clearly mastered the breadless arts, middle-class Lipochka, in the matchmaker's picturesque metaphor, manages to write at best "like an elephant crawling on its belly" (Act II, Sc. 7; I, 117), and her achievement in the other arts is comparable. Both girls resist their parents, but Lipochka's opposition has greater cause. "If you knew what life here is like," she says to Podkhalyuzin. "Mama makes every day a fast day, and Father, when he isn't drunk, keeps silent, and when he is, beats everybody and everything he gets hold of. . . . If I married a gentleman, I could leave this house and forget it all" (Act III, Sc. 5; I, 135).

Marrying a gentleman is but a girlish fantasy, however, and at her father's dictate Lipochka accepts his business associate, a man of her own class. The great Russian critic Nikolay Dobrolyubov, who thought the depiction of the middle-class milieu the innovative achievement of the young Ostrovsky, termed this world "the dark kingdom" *(temnoe tsarstvo)* in his famous article of 1859 of that title. He also adopted Ostrovsky's own later word, *samodur*, for a domestic tyrant like Bolshov, and *samodurstvo* for his unenlightened use of his absolute power over his family and business.

Interestingly enough, Ostrovsky's first *samodur* Bolshov is hardly typical: though his aim in giving his children his possessions is sly and selfish, he places himself in their power like a Russian King Lear. Though Lear's misfortunes are mitigated by the love of at least three human beings, not a single loving heart appears in the consistently dark world of Ostrovsky's first play. Dobrolyubov discusses its literary depiction as truth which, as such, must arouse moral judgment, and hence an impulse to rebel against so senseless a way of life. Thus Dobrolyubov sees Ostrovsky's first play as a critique of social reality rather than a literary creation.

In exposing corrupt business practices Ostrovsky, first among classic Russian dramatists, assayed the theme of capitalism, which in 1861, with the emancipation of the serfs, became the basis of the Russian economy. Both Bolshov and Podkhalyuzin are already gamblers with their capital, and the younger man may be interpreted as actually the hero of the play because he wins at the game. Bolshov understands the nature of the mere paper values with which they are dealing: "Always one debtor's note and then another!" he says. "And what's a note? Well, it's paper, and that's the whole thing" (Act I, Sc. 12; I, 105).

Podkhalyuzin first acquires capital through marriage, and so Lipochka embodies another important theme of Ostrovsky's work, the woman sold in marriage. Her fiancé values her "educated" accomplishments as part of the assets he is acquiring. The capitalist Vasilkov in Ostrovsky's postemancipation play *Easy Money (Beshennye den'gi,* 1870) will buy in his bride her social accomplishments if only for their value in advancing his career, though he is in love with her as well. Neither one of the young couple in *A Family Affair* is in love with the other, just as neither feels any pangs of conscience. Podkhalyuzin transcends his: "They say you must have a conscience. Of course, . . . but how are we to understand this? Anyone has a conscience when he's dealing with a good person, but if this person cheats others, then where's the conscience in cheating him!" (Act II, Sc. 3; I, 109). Clearly Podkhalyuzin need not reproach himself for cheating Bolshov, for the latter taught him to swindle. Podkhalyuzin, in turn, inculcates ruthlessness in the office boy Tishka, who no doubt will one day serve him as he has Bolshov.

The secondary figures in A Family Affair—Lipochka's doting mother, the matchmaker, and the scrivener Rispolozhensky—are lambs to the slaughter of Podkhalyuzin's ruthlessness. Their mechanical consistency of character is epitomized by the scrivener's set response to every invitation to a drink: "Don't mind if I do!"; repetition of the phrase raises it to a device reminiscent of Dickens. The comedy inherent in the repetition, though, makes the character seem wooden, just as Lipochka is little more than a puppet with the set responses of a spoiled child. Only the matchmaker comes alive, partly through her rich popular speech, partly through her pride peculiar to the people: "In what am I worse than she?" (Act II, Sc. 7; I, 117), she asks, referring to Mrs. Bolshov. The clerk Podkhalyuzin, too, despite his outward servility, believes in himself: "Why shouldn't I marry her?" he thinks aloud of Lipochka. "By what reason am I not a human being?" (Act II, Sc. 3; I, 109).

Not even the play's all too obvious mechanisms—exposition, extended monologues, conclusion with a direct address to the audience—can hamper the vivid forward impulse of its simple plot line: a hero on his way up in the world. Podkhalyuzin's closing invitation to the audience has been criticized as an "open" or inconclusive ending, but its very openness rather marks the clerk's new start in the role of employer. The ending represents an ongoing continuum, as in reality.

In sum, this success story of an emerging class is at the same time an exposure of the shady tactics of business. For the first time in classic Russian drama money is the driving force of the plot, and the middle class alone is the subject. Lipochka's marriage establishes another important Ostrovskian theme. Beside the two themes of money and marriage, the minimally complicated plot and the traditional mechanics of the play with its "open ending" are characteristic of the early Ostrovsky.

During the playwright's lifetime A Family Affair was by number of performances his fourth most popular play, though from his death until 1917 it fell only in the upper half of his most produced plays and since 1917 has been even less frequently staged. It has been included in several English anthologies of Ostrovsky's plays by reason of the historic novelty of its subject. Certainly it is not one of his best.

II *The Marriage Market:* A Poor Bride *(1852)*

In Ostrovsky's next important play, *Bednaia nevesta* (A Poor Bride), the second theme of *A Family Affair* comes to the fore: the dependence of women and the marriage of convenience. Maria Andreevna, or Masha—the poor bride of the title—believes the protestations of love made her by her suitors Milashin and Merich, who woo her despite her lack of a dowry. She even thinks herself in love with the latter, until he proves untrue. She must marry a man with business sense to bring order into the tangled affairs which she and her mother have inherited from her father, so she sadly accepts a vulgar and elderly civil servant, Benevolensky, hoping that even without love she can make a good home and family.

The suitors Milashin and Merich both prove to be unworthy men. Milashin (Mr. Very Nice), far from being the Milon (Mr. Nice) whom the heroine will inevitably marry, as in Denis Fonvizin's eighteenth-century comedy *The Minor,* denounces his rival Merich to her only to get ahead of him, and not, as he claims, for love of her. Merich does not truly love Masha either, but merely seeks in her another conquest. Very early the critic Apollon Grigorev, who in a survey of Russian literature in 1851 recognized the play's greatness, also perceived the irony of Ostrovsky's treatment of the allusive names once associated with Romantic heroes: Pushkin and "Lermontov are not to blame that types, which at a certain time were genuine and poetic, grow petty and common from constant repetition."[1] The modern critic Vladimir Lakshin explicitly links Merich with Lermontov's archetype of the Romantic hero, Pechorin:

In Merich Ostrovsky wanted to compromise the artificial Romantic pose, to discredit it from the standpoint of real life, reason, common sense. Merich is the faded, dwindled Lermontovian hero Grushnitsky pretending to be Pechorin. Even his name carries with it a kind of literary allusion. Its stem is the name "Mary" (by the way, Merich calls Maria Andreevna "Mary" ["Meri" in Russian, like the princess with whose affections "a hero of our time" baits his rival] at their meetings), while the ending "-ich" is one usual

with Lermontov (Vulich, Zvezdich). In the first version the literary polemic
in the play was still clearer: . . . Ostrovsky had Maria Andreevna hold a
book by Lermontov in her hand, while he had Merich (at first Zorich) tell in
purest Pechorinese about easy conquests of women's hearts.[2]

The plot is not resolved as one might expect from the names, for
Masha marries neither of the young men, but the middle-aged
Benevolensky (Mr. Benevolent), recommended to her mother by
Dobrotvorsky (Mr. Do-good). Benevolensky, too, belies his name,
for it is not benevolence but his own material interest which
prompts him to seek a beautiful and educated bride, and in the
process to abandon his mistress of five years' standing.

No plot contrivances compel Masha to accept her fate. She sees
through Merich's pretense at love without Milashin's disclosures
about his rival. Nor is she deceived about her future husband, for
she knows that he is "coarse and takes bribes." But she does delude
herself about her possible influence over him: "They say a woman
can do a lot if she wants to. . . . I feel that there is strength in me. I
shall make him love, respect and obey me. And finally the children.
I shall live for the children" (Act V, Sc. 5; I, 271).

If Masha is not deluded about Benevolensky, his abandoned
mistress also knows about Masha and yet does not intrigue to
prevent the marriage. She even urges her former lover to be good to
his bride, and promises him she will not interfere. Thus freed from
the possibility of a scandal, Benevolensky asks the waiter for a drink,
despite having pretended to Masha to give up drinking. Though he
takes only sherry—not vodka, as formerly—it is clear that Masha
can hardly hope to reform him. But at least the couple is well-off, as
the women bystanders at the wedding enviously remark.

Like *A Family Affair*, *A Poor Bride* is open-ended, suggesting the
continuation of the action after the play's close. Nor, without plot
twists, is there any untwisting or denouement of complicated lines
of action. Such simplicity creates an even more dispassionate illu-
sion of reality than the somewhat tendentious exposure of social evil
in *A Family Affair*, which inspired revulsion for the conditions it
exposed. Here one feels only melancholy at a woman's fate if she is
poor like the poor bride. Masha's maid says, "You have to realize
how things go in the world: if you're rich, you are looked up to by
all; if you're poor, nobody pays any attention to you. That means you
don't need to be a person, only to have money" (Act I, Sc. 5; I, 198).

Masha, too, knows: "Even a monster imagines he has a right to woo me; he even thinks he's doing me a favor because, as he says, she's a poor bride. Another thinks he can simply bargain for me as for an object" (ibid.; I, 197).

Seemingly Dobrolyubov's schematization of conflict in Ostrovsky's work applies to such enslavement by poverty: "The dramatic collisions and catastrophes in Ostrovsky's plays all arise from the confrontation of two parties—the old and the young, the rich and the poor, the authoritarians and their underlings."[3] Norman Henley has expanded the list of such possible conflicts in Ostrovsky's work.[4] Actually, however, Masha is not oppressed by any *samodur* unless by the *samodurstvo* of society itself which assigned women an underling's role.[5] On the other hand, a burgeoning capitalism will compel men in later Ostrovsky plays to sell themselves in marriage as well.

Ostrovsky's *A Poor Bride* reflects a broad perception of woman's condition: the classes and the masses of both mistress and maid, the women's chorus at the end, and the demi-mondaine, Dunia the mistress. These last describe the state of women in love. Benevolensky's mistress confesses: "True, I loved him once. . . . Of course, I knew some good at his hands—more tears" (Act V, Sc. 9; I, 276). A voice from the women bystanders at the wedding describes the married state: "Another man, a good man, likes us to please him. They come home drunk, of course, more often than not, and like us to take care of them—won't let anyone else come near them." The last word, then—"poor bride"—has come to mean in the end not so much "impoverished" as "poor thing" (I, 279).

Besides depicting a broader spectrum of women, Ostrovsky's second play expands its view of men to include not just businessmen, but civil servants, the two beaux Milashin and Merich with their aristocratic airs, as well as a poor student, Khorkov, who is also in love with Masha. No one is a villain, not even the careerist Benevolensky, an all too ordinary man of little soul.

Like *A Family Affair*, this second play could not be produced at first, though Ostrovsky read it in Moscow circles beginning in 1851, and upon its publication in the *Moskvityanin* in February 1852 Grigorev issued his famous pronouncement: "The question from whom to expect a new word [in Russian literature] can already be answered directly: . . . in this new work . . . we find new hopes for art."[6] Vasily Botkin, however, in a letter to Turgenev found the play's new objectivity cold and dry. Nikolay Chernyshevsky thought the play lacking in any new idea and too restricted in dealing with private, not public, life. Dobrolyubov saw it as further evidence of *samodurstvo.*

After his first bold praise, even Grigorev criticized the play for "an absence of economy in its conception, its structure."[7] The subplot of the student Khorkov's unrequited love for Masha, which remains undeveloped, is said to reflect both Grigorev's love for Antonina and Ostrovsky's interest in Zinaida, two of the five Korsh sisters, in whose home Ostrovsky and his friends visited frequently. Indeed, the situation of the widow Korsh with her marriageable daughters, and especially one daughter, Lyubov's, match with a coarse and—as it proved—corrupt law professor provided the "slice of life" for *A Poor Bride.* Surely the playwright's own involvement with the Korsh circle—as in a *roman à clef,* the figures and feelings of the play are identifiable—pushed him on to completion of the long, not yet quite purposeful work on this second full-length play.

Some years later, in 1859, the critic Alexander Druzhinin summarized the favorable view of the play: "Though the beauty of *A Poor Bride* is less accessible to the masses than that of *A Family Affair,* its content is closer to life generally. . . .The author's success and progress are seen in the creation of characters as valid types . . . almost all [of whom] are our brothers and sisters."[8] Indeed, this young woman, educated for nothing but the marriage market, hoping against hope to find fulfillment in a loveless marriage to a man of indifferent character, comes inexplicably to life in this haunting play.

III   *Concession to Censorship or Slavophile Deviation?*

Ostrovsky's next play, *Ne v svoi sani ne sadis' (Stay in Your own Lane,* literally, "Don't Get in a Sleigh Not Your Own"), produced in 1853, was his first work to reach the stage. Indeed, it was so successful that *A Poor Bride* was also staged the same year. Ostrovsky's favorable presentation of the principal characters in *Stay in Your Own Lane* and in his next two plays led to the charge that he had abandoned his critical stance and converted to Slavophilism, or the love of the Russian people and of old Slavic ways without benefit of Western upper-class culture.[9]

The play concerns a wealthy shopkeeper's daughter, who elopes with an aristocrat who wants only the girl's money. When the nobleman learns that her father will disinherit her for marrying him, he sends her home unwed and unharmed. The fiancé from her own class favored by her father shows his true love by disregarding her apparent disgrace and happily marrying her anyway. The greatness of heart of this "hero in shirtsleeves"—as Nikolay Nekrasov, editor of the liberal journal *Sovremennik* (The Contemporary) called him—the wisdom of the shopkeeper father and the realistic presentation for the first time in the theater of ordinary Russian people, stimulated a lively discussion.

Apollon Grigorev and Nekrasov denied that there was any political purpose in Ostrovsky's unfavorable comparison of the aristocrat with the simple suitor. True, the positive portraits of those men of the people, the father and son-in-law, conformed to the Slavophile orientation of the *Moskvityanin,* in which Ostrovsky's first three plays appeared, and which the playwright had joined as editor in 1850. Nor did Ostrovsky continue to push for production of *A Family Affair,* with its sharp criticism of Russian business people. As he wrote Pogodin on September 30, 1853, "I do not wish to make only enemies for myself."[10] *Stay in Your Own Lane,* he continued, displayed his new "bent," "that a Russian should rather experience joy at seeing himself on stage than sorrow. Reformers will be found without us. To have the right to reform the people without offending them, you must show them that you find some good in them; that is what I'm doing now. . . ."[11]

Ostrovsky shared a belief in the goodness of Russian people with the so-called "young editorial board," whom he attracted to the *Moskvityanin,* and of whom Apollon Grigorev and he were the stars. However, the younger men were more moderate in their Slavophilism than the magazine's owner, Pogodin, and Ostrovsky's play does excoriate *samodurstvo* in the heroine's father despite his patriarchal goodheartedness. Of the daughter Dobrolyubov wrote in "The Dark Kingdom": "A person brainwashed under the influence of the *samodurstvo* weighing upon him may against his will unconsciously commit any kind of crime, and perish simply out of stupidity and lack of independence."[12] So even the good *samodur's* daughter, brought up to love and obey, commits the "crime" of elopement, from which indeed she nearly perishes.

The three so-called Slavophile plays, beginning with *Stay in Your Own Lane,* differ considerably among themselves in plot, characters, and setting. *Ne tak zhivi kak khochetsia* (Don't Live as You Like It, 1855) plays on folk notions of the devil in connection with a young married man's temptation to enter upon an illicit love affair

with a hearty girl of the people. *Bednost' ne porok* (Poverty's No
Vice, 1854) depicts the wealthy milieu of a businessman who hopes
to marry his daughter to a millionaire manufacturer. The father's
ill-advised effort to ascend into a higher class is defeated both by the
daughter's love for his own employee and by the simple humanity of
his brother, whom he has wronged. The brother, Lyubim
Tortsov—ne'er-do-well, failure, and drinker—afterwards became a
folk hero, and a favorite role in the theater. Ostrovsky's friend the
actor Prov Sadovsky of the Moscow Maly Theater acted the part so
impressively that Grigorev dedicated an ode to Sadovsky's Lyubim,
drunk, but with a "pure Russian heart."[13] Lyubim's complexity, his
guiltless guilt, caused that great actor of an earlier age, Mikhail
Shchepkin, to attempt the role near the end of his life in 1855.
Indeed, the success of this third play made it clear that Ostrovsky
had arrived in the theater.

Though the three "Slavophile" plays can hardly be considered
great literature, neither can they be condemned as concessions to
public taste for the sake of success. Rather they reveal Ostrovsky's
talent for representing characters from the common people, his
interest in their lives and feelings. In particular, they demonstrate
his extraordinary gift for recreating ordinary speech. They thus
enlarged the domain of the Russian drama, and also proved Ostrovsky's work was not only stageworthy but could arouse actors'
enthusiasm.

IV   *The Matchmaker's Farce: The Balzaminov Trilogy*

If the figure of Milashin in *A Poor Bride* constitutes a wry
commentary on a predecessor from classic eighteenth-century Russian comedy, and Merich in the same play parodies Lermontov's
Pechorin, then it is not surprising that the Balzaminov trilogy
should both hark back to the greatest master of Russian comedy,
Gogol, and also mock his work. Yet the farcical comedy of the three
plays, so different from Ostrovsky's earlier dramas, seems hardly to
have been understood at the time they appeared. Indeed, the
editors of the journals in which the first two plays of the trilogy came
out appear not to have been favorably impressed by them:
Prazdnichnyi son—do obeda (The Holiday Dream Comes True by
Noon) appeared in Nikolay Nekrasov's *Sovremennik* for February
1857; and *Svoi sobaki gryzutsia, chuzaia ne pristavai* (Our Dogs Are
at Each Other, Keep Yours Off) was published in Alexey Pisemsky's

Biblioteka dlya chteniya (Reading Library) in March 1861. Consequently, the final play of the trilogy—*Za chem poidesh', to i naidesh'* (What You Seek You'll Find, also called The Marriage of Balzaminov)—appeared in still a third journal, Fedor Dostoevsky's *Vremya* (Time) for September 1861. Moreover, Dostoevsky wrote Ostrovsky an enthusiastic letter about the last play, saying that his brother and he had laughed at it until their sides ached, that it was a "delight."[14]

The hero of all three plays—Misha Balzaminov, a poor civil service clerk who is not very bright—dreams of making a rich marriage. In the first play a matchmaker introduces him to the rich girl Kapitolina Nichkina, who caught sight of him as she sat at her window dreaming of a Prince Charming. Predisposed to mistake Balzaminov for her prince, she is warned by her sensible uncle that her harmless suitor will only squander her wealth, and allows herself rather to be persuaded to marry a young man of the uncle's choosing who is intelligent enough to put her capital to work.

Thus the first Balzaminov play is the reverse of a dream come true, in which the unheroic simpleton is pure enough in heart to win the heroine. Instead Balzaminov emerges in the common-sense view as a hymeneal predator bent on acquiring unearned wealth and enjoyment. The uncle from afar—true, not from Siberia, as in classic eighteenth-century comedy, but only from nearby Kolomna—inverts the role of *raisonneur*, the personage who in Classical comedy rights wrongs and brings young lovers together: instead he prevents the union for practical reasons.

Among the play's tried and true comic devices are its speaking names. The matchmaker's first name, Akulina (the shark), alludes to her cupidity in seizing on rewards for her services, while her patronymic, Gavrilovna (Gabriella), associates her with the archangel, as if the marriage proposals she brings were comparable to the annunciation. Her patronymic, she confesses, has been distorted into the nickname "Govorilikha" (Mrs. Garrulous).

Pisemsky even thought it a worn-out vaudeville gag when the hero first appears on stage yowling in pain, his hair alight from the curling iron with which the cook has sought in the kitchen to embellish him. The ensuing exchange between mother and son exemplifies another comic device, the puns of the dialogue:

Mother: Za delo. [Let's get down to business.]
Son: Kakoe, zadela! [What business, she hurt me!] (Tabl. I, Sc. 2; II, 113)

In addition to puns, the matchmaker's malapropisms help constitute the unashamedly comic dialogue of the first play.

And yet, for all its stock devices, the first play derived its germ of inspiration from the real life of the Beyond-the-River District, as appears from comparable moments in the scenes *Ne soshlis' kharakterami* (Incompatible Characters, 1858). Here too a poor civil service clerk dreams the all too human dream of the easy life gained by marrying money. Dostoevsky found the matchmaker so true to life that he wrote: "I've seen her a thousand times. I was personally acquainted with her; she used to come to see us when I lived in Moscow during the first ten years of my life. I remember her."[15]

In the second Balzaminov play—*Our Dogs Are at Each Other, Keep Yours Off*—Balzaminov again emerges the loser. Through the matchmaker he woos Mme. Intriguing, who listens to him only in order to take revenge on her true love, Pavlin Ustrashimov (Mr. Peacock Thunderbuss), whom she thinks she has seen courting another woman one day. But Balzaminov assures her that Ustrashimov, his office coworker, spent all of the day in question at work. So Balzaminov reunites the two lovers, and thus destroys his own chance for happiness.

In this play, too, Balzaminov is satirized. He cuts a ridiculous figure when Ustrashimov so terrifies him by a letter threatening reprisals if he goes near Intriguing that it takes all his mother's encouragement to make Balzaminov meet his intended. His ultimate stupidity in telling the truth reverses the Parsifal fairy-tale cliché whereby the pure fool wins out.

Much of the linguistic fun in this play occurs in a briefing which the mother gives her son to upgrade his vocabulary for conversation with his lady love: she professes to teach him pigeon French, with hilarious results.

However, from the last play of the trilogy, *The Marriage of Balzaminov*, the hero emerges crowned with success at last. A retired officer asks Misha's aid in eloping with one of two rich sisters, promising him the hand of the other in return. Though the matchmaker offers marriage with the plump, wealthy widow Belotelova (Mrs. Whitebody), Misha feels obliged to help his friend. The officer elopes successfully, leaving Misha to decoy his bride's vengeful brothers. Misha goes over the garden wall, only to fall into the nettles of Belotelova's garden. She takes his precipitate arrival as assent to her proposal. So he returns home elated, with two prospective brides, and even thinks of marrying both as he and his mother sit in the twilight, dreaming of wealth. But the matchmaker tilts the balance in favor of her client, and Misha ends happily in the wealthy widow's lush embrace.

However reprehensible Misha's predatory enterprise, and however ridiculous his management of it, an appealing aura attaches to this poor fool, as to Gogol's hero in *The Overcoat*. N. E. Berg, whose account decades later launched the legend that Gogol had passed an encouraging note to Ostrovsky, also raises the issue of literary succession. Of the memo which cannot be found Berg says: "This document is all the more important because even in those years the question was widely discussed whether Ostrovsky represented the continuation of the Gogolian 'natural school' with its critical relationship to reality, or whether his work was that 'new word,' as A. A. Grigorev put it, which had no connection with the Gogolian tradition, and was even consciously opposed to it."[16] Peter Pletnev, a friend of Princess Evdokia Rostopchina, the supposed transmitter of the memo, unhesitatingly assigned *A Family Affair* to the Gogolian tradition. With this very play, however, as with *A Poor Bride*—which Grigorev had hailed as prophetic of "a new word" in Russian literature—the playwright struck his contemporaries as an innovator. Yet the Balzaminov trilogy is closer to Gogol's comedies, even when it parodies them, than any other early play or plays by Ostrovsky.

True, all three Balzaminov plays bear the designation "Pictures of Russian life." Yet, like Gogol's plays, they are comedies in the tradition of ancient convention. According to the French philosopher Henri Bergson, we laugh at, not with, someone who slips on a banana peel, and the overwhelmingly comic Balzaminov plays lack deeper significance because we do not empathize with the hero. He is ridiculous in misfortune when, escaping his pursuers over the garden wall, he lands in the nettles. So Bobchinsky in Gogol's *Inspector General* provokes our laughter when he, too, falls on his face as the door opens, behind which he has been eavesdropping on the mayor and Khlestakov in *The Inspector General*. In Ostrovsky, farcical falls of this sort occur only in the Balzaminov plays, and only there is farcical fear felt, too: for example, Balzaminov's fear of Ustrashimov, comparable to the mayor's and Khlestakov's mutual terror at their first meeting.

Further traits link Balzaminov with Khlestakov. Both seek their own advantage, but neither is very bright. Khlestakov needs Osip's advice to leave in good time, while Balzaminov is counseled by his mother. Both are extravagant dreamers. Both assume the lover's attitude, though quite without feeling, as a proper pose in society; both overfulfill the norm by conquering two possible brides, and must be constrained to take but one. By laughably exceeding the norm, both imply criticism of it.

Balzaminov's repeated loss of the girl makes him resemble the traditional stock character of the commedia dell'arte, Pierrot, who loses Columbine to Harlequin. Pushkin's friend the poet Peter Vyazemsky once complained: "Where are our Polichinelles [the Pierrot of the Italian commedia dell'arte]?"[17] In Balzaminov Ostrovsky recreated the constant dupe, a Russian Misha to match the Pierrot of the commedia dell'arte. Further, the personages of the trilogy—the hero, his mother, their maid, and the matchmaker—pass from one play to another, just as the set roles of the commedia remain the same through many variants of plot and situation. Both Ustrashimov and the eloping officer show traits of the commedia Braggadochio. Balzaminov's fear of being beaten recurs in folk theater from Punch and Judy to Falstaff in the laundry basket, while his fall into the nettles reminds one of Cherubino's landing on the flower pot in *The Marriage of Figaro,* also a commedia descendant.

Not just characters and plot, but certain technical devices as well are obvious clichés of theater tradition. Thus the mother's monologue at the start of the first and second plays resembles the direct address of information to the audience in medieval comedy, or a folk comedy by Hans Sachs. Again, the dialogue between Intriguing and her friend in Scene 2 of the second play serves as exposition, like the conversation with a confidant in French classic theater.

In contrast to such age-old conventions of characters and situations, the setting of the plays is contemporary, real-life Moscow. When Balzaminov's mother dreams that her son is summoning her to China, he immediately brings her dream down to earth by relating it to "the Chinese city," as the oldest inner city of Moscow is still called; after all, that is where Belotelova has her store. If the matchmaker's plans for realizing the hero's fantastic dream of wealth are couched in folk and fairy-tale language, the fairy tale comes true amid the petty-bourgeois conventions and mindless superstitions of middle-class Moscow. In the fool's paradise of a fat widow's arms Balzaminov finds the happiness he is incapable of reckoning exactly in rubles. Ostrovsky has managed to incorporate folk material in this ironic farce better than in his serious, Slavophile-oriented plays;

with laughter more effectively than with Realistic portrayal he has unmasked ignorance and indolence, poverty, and superstition in the middle-class life of nascent capitalism.

The gifted comedian of the Alexandrinsky Theater Alexander Martynov created Balzaminov unforgettably on stage in 1857 but did not live to continue that role in the two later plays. Perhaps for that reason some critics found the continuation superfluous and suggested combining the three plays in one. The director of the Moscow Taganka Theater, Yury Lyubimov, in his 1973 "composition" *Benefis* (*Benefit Performance*), combined motifs from the tragedy *The Storm* (1861) and the Balzaminov comedies instead. The success of such a combination surely shows more than just the compatibility of two works from the same period of Ostrovsky's life. Rather such tragedy and comedy in one represent a quintessence of the Ostrovskian genius.

CHAPTER 3

First Mature Plays: The Major Issues Unchanged

I *Business and/or Marriage as Usual:* A Profitable Post *(1857)*

THE assignment of the Balzaminov trilogy to Ostrovsky's early
plays and of *Dokhodnoe mesto (A Profitable Post),* written in
the same year, to the mature plays is somewhat arbitrary. In fact
Ostrovsky's plays show remarkable maturity from the start, yet each
is in some way peculiar unto itself, as if the young playwright had
with each tried a different direction in his search for the correct one.
Perhaps this alone justifies the designation "early," for with each
play here called "mature," Ostrovsky takes a step forward on the
single path he has by now found on his way to the peak of his
profession. In this third half-decade of his career the two major
themes of the power of money and the place of women continue
paramount; they are equally important, and even conjoined, in
A Profitable Post.

Two sisters, Yulinka and Polina, have been prepared for marriage
so strictly by their mother Kukushkina, widow of a civil servant, that
they can hardly wait to be married and freed from her dominance.
Yulinka's liberation by marriage to her unloved suitor Belogubov
awaits only the mother's consent, which is contingent on his promo-
tion to a post with salary sufficient to support a wife. Zhadov, whom
Polina loves, has the better prospects as the nephew of the high
official Vyshnevsky, under whom both young men serve. Belogubov, however, who has learned to take bribes from the chief
clerk, a master of the art, is promoted to the post both young men
need, while Zhadov loses even the job he had because he flaunts his
honesty to his uncle's face. Zhadov had already obtained Kukushkina's consent to marry Polina on the basis of his prospects alone.
Now, though he takes on three odd jobs, Polina and he suffer

poverty. Yulinka gives her sister a pretty hat from her own superfluity and advises Polina to threaten leaving her husband if he will not follow the general practice of bribe-taking. Zhadov capitulates, and Polina and he go to ask pardon of his uncle, and beg for his old job back. They find that Vyshnevsky has been dismissed from high office for malfeasance and suffered a fatal stroke. The young couple reaffirm their love, and their conviction that honesty must after all triumph over corruption.

The parallel couples—the idealists Zhadov and Polina and the pragmatists Belogubov and Yulinka—are not the only embodiments of high-minded principle versus worldly compromise: Vyshnevsky and his wife are antithetical. He stands for graft, until he is finally called to account, while she stands for integrity, deploring the widespread permissiveness in high society and high office.

The other pair of oldsters—the chief clerk Yusov and the mother Kukushkina—believe only in two principles: the young should obey their elders, and the good is what succeeds. When Zhadov refuses to follow his uncle's deviant path, Yusov calls him disobedient. Kukushkina, too, disapproves of Zhadov's newfangled ideals, finding it incredible that a civil servant should live only on his salary and refuse bribes. Such conduct can only offend "good people," for bribes, she says, are "not bribes, but gratitude" (Act IV, Sc. 4; II, 87).

If Kukushkina's notions of honesty are remarkable, her ideas on the role of women are even more so. The fact that her daughters have learned nothing at school is unimportant to her. Instead, she sternly instills in them the art of luring a husband. Thus, when Belogubov is announced, she commands: "Sit in your places. Yulinka, drop your shawl a little to show your right shoulder" (Act II, Sc. 2; II, 61). The mother further teaches her daughters her own ethic of the wife as a parasite who forces her husband to bring home ever more money to keep her in idleness and luxury. The wife does not work in the house, or even supervise the servants; all she does is attend the theater, dressed in the height of fashion, or visit friends. No wonder that, as Zhadov wears himself out to earn a subsistence wage, Polina is, as he says, "always without work, always sitting with hands folded" (Act IV, Sc. 5; II, 89).

Finally, Kukushkina instructs her daughter to use the weapon of Lysistrata in bringing her husband round. Does Polina's threat—and she admits later it was only a threat—to leave Zhadov accomplish what a year of poverty could not do: force him to surrender his principles? What a picture, then, this play paints of women's insidious power from within, and of its abuse! The two young couples are believable characters, though Zhadov's speaking name (Mr. Eager) tends to type him, and the mother's, Kukushkina (Mrs. Cuckoo), renders her ridiculous. She, though, is hardly human; rather she represents the whipping post of female power against which the play directs its satire. With the airs of a general, she musters her daughters like troops before their sally into the marriage market. She directs the strategy by which Polina brings her husband to heel. She creates conditions which make a wife a bottomless maw greedy for material advantage. Not for a moment is her feigned grief believable when she consents to Zhadov's marrying Polina:

Kukushkina: I confess it's hard for me to part with her. She is my favorite daughter . . . (Covers her face with her handkerchief.)
(Zhadov and Polina kiss her hand. Belogubov brings her a chair. She sits down.)
Yusov: You are a real mother, Felisata Gerasimovna.
Kukushkina: Yes, I can flatter myself to be that. (With feeling.) No, bringing up daughters is an ungrateful task! You rear them, cuddle them close, and then give them away to a stranger, . . . are left alone in the world . . . awful! (Covers her eyes with her handkerchief.)
Belogubov: Mamma dear, we won't leave you.
Polina and Yulinka (together): Mamma dear, we won't leave you.
(End of Act II; II, 70)

The scene is a caricature of affection with the repetition of her gesture with her handkerchief and her daughters' protestations.

Yusov, on the contrary, is wholly genuine in his unashamed submission to things as they are. He even celebrates his rise in the world through bribe-taking by dancing Russian-style at the inn and making a speech to the opening of a bottle of champagne: "I have a happy heart, a calm soul! . . . I shall even dance on the square in front of everyone. Passersby will say: 'Obviously this man is dancing because he has a clean conscience!' " (Act III, Sc. 3; II, 78).

The uncle, too—Vyshnevsky—who has reached the top by large-scale gift, suffers neither pangs of conscience nor public embarrassment. "There is no public opinion, . . ." he tells his nephew. "As long as you're not caught, you're not a thief" (Act I, Sc. 9; II, 52). But Zhadov, who believes in both personal conscience and the development of enlightened public opinion as a check on dishonesty, has the last word in the debate: "I await the time when the bribetaker will fear the judgment of public opinion more than the criminal courts" (Act V, Sc. 4; II, 110).

Aside from uncle-nephew debates on official corruption, Vyshnevsky and his wife also engage in acrimonious exchanges on the marriage of convenience. Such discussions are infrequent in Ostrovsky, for they amount to the direct exposition of ideas, comparable to Shavian preachment.

The Vyshnevskys' discussions occur in what the Soviet critic Abram Shtein calls "the strange frame of the play—Vyshnevsky's relations with his wife."[1] They are strange because they are melodramatic and peripheral to the main action. In the last act Vyshnevsky's wife recounts her prehistory at length: in love with another, she was "bought" in marriage from her relatives by Vyshnevsky "as slaves are bought in Turkey" (Act V, Sc. 3; II, 106). Since he failed to win her heart after marriage despite his lavish gifts, he jealously hunted to death the man she had once loved. But for the uncle's fall—which like a deus ex machina saves Zhadov from betraying his principles—Vyshnevsky is unessential to the action. Both his and Zhadov's expositions on government corruption and the sale of women in marriage are, to say the least, undramatic.

Beside the Vyshnevskys, two other characters—they appear only in the central third act—are essential only to the play's argument, not to its action. At an inn a year after his wedding Zhadov meets an old friend, Mykin, now a teacher, who ekes out an honest living only because he had abandoned his intention of marrying the girl he loved. Mykin quotes the proverb: a loner isn't poor, but if you're poor, then go it alone. Zhadov's other encounter at the inn is with Dosuzhev, a university man and jurist, too, who is also too honest to take bribes. Instead of entering the civil service, he writes petitions for clients. However profitable it may be, though, his work has so undermined his self-respect that he has taken to drink. He even sends Zhadov, usually a teetotaler, home drunk.

Some moments before, Zhadov had refused to join in the toasts of his former colleagues, though Belogubov, celebrating an unusually big bribe, repeatedly invites him to do so. Belogubov insists he owes everything to Yusov, who, righteous in his wrong-doing, even formulates an ethic of bribe-taking.

Bribery was not a new subject in the Russian theater. Gogol's *Inspector General*, which dealt with this theme, had won the approval of Nicholas I, who sent his officials to see the play for the moral lesson it taught. The removal of Vyshnevsky from office also gives Ostrovsky's play a moral ending. Why then did *A Profitable Post* have to wait six years for permission to be performed? The Soviet critic Efim Kholodov suggests that it was Ostrovsky's depiction not so much of bribery as such as of its universality which made the play dangerous in the censor's view.

The hero's unheroic capitulation amounts to an especially telling criticism of bribery, according to Kholodov, who asks:

Why did Ostrovsky put his hero through his moral surrender? So as to show that the hero of his play is altogether unheroic. So as to demonstrate that the way of life he [Zhadov] observed around him inevitably destroys honest people, and brings them to their knees. So as to show up . . . a way of life in which a man must be a hero if he is not to become a rogue.[2]

Ostrovsky's contemporaries recognized the play's depth and power. In a letter to Vasily Botkin Tolstoy called it Ostrovsky's best to date, adding: "Just like *A Family Affair* it makes a strong protest against contemporary ways."[3] Both Tolstoy and Pisemsky sensed the contrived falseness of the Vyshnevskys. Chernyshevsky, while praising some of the same points as the others, added his appreciation of Belogubov, who, though dishonest in taking bribes, at least uses them for the benefit of his wife and others. Dobrolyubov lauded Ostrovsky's perspective on officialdom from the human and family side. Grigorev found tragedy in the relegation to meaningless employment of society's most valuable members, such as Dosuzhev, and in the falseness of a society in which "untruth has become the very essence of life, a society in which even the sense of any kind of truth has been lost."[4] Grigorev was undoubtedly right in his pessimistic perception, for the open ending in which Zhadov expresses hope for a change in public opinion is no more believable than the poor bride's hopes in the open ending of the earlier play.

In a production of *A Profitable Post* soon after 1917 Vsevolod Meyerhold gave the play a revolutionary thrust by emphasizing the tyranny of unenlightened oldsters over idealistic young people, and the submission to authority they required in the name of respect. So Yusov was made conspicuously servile to his superior, and he prefers the complacent Belogubov over Zhadov for the profitable post because he thinks the nephew disrespectful for holding views different from his uncle's. Meyerhold also made almost a symbol of perverse bourgeois luxury out of the hat which Yulinka hands down to her sister. The hat provides the stimulus for Polina's leaving her husband when in the pride of their poverty he insists that she return it. Her departure, in turn, brings him to abandon his principles—as if a hat for a man's wife could cause corruption in high places. The possibility of such a variant reading proves the richness of the play's material.

The symmetry of the play's structure is quite classic. Framed by the first and last act at Vyshnevsky's, the second and fourth acts show Kukushkina and her girls, and the third act, Zhadov at the crossroads. Like a school model of dramatic structure, the fourth act introduces the mandatory unexpected element: Polina's revolt and Zhadov's recantation, this last epitomized in a bitter song. Though the play may be considered lacking in economy because of its many episodic characters, it may also be called too well-made by reason of its symmetrical structure.

The play's conclusion can be criticized as indecisively open-ended because it leaves Polina and Zhadov with ideals a bit the worse for wear and no means of realizing them. Yet the conclusion can also be criticized as contrived because with Vyshnevsky struck down vice is punished in exemplary fashion. A playwright who can so satisfy both moralists and Realists in the end has surely progressed in his craft. Certainly *A Profitable Post* poses still valid and complex questions about the lives of ordinary human beings. Consequently it has deservedly remained in the modern repertory among Ostrovsky's mature plays.

II   *The Stereotype for Years to Come: Nikolay Dobrolyubov's Assessment of the First Decade*

The critic Nikolay Chernyshevsky, who early noted Ostrovsky's work, wrote in the year of its publication that *A Profitable Post* was set in "a circle having nothing in common with the business world."[5] *A Poor Bride*, too, had described not business men, but civil servants, as had the Balzaminov plays. Yet the critic Nikolay Dobrolyubov singled out a characteristic, above all, of wealthy businessmen, protagonists of a majority of Ostrovsky's early plays, as the hallmark of all his plays of the first decade. Reviewing a two-volume edition of Ostrovsky's work published in 1859, Dobrolyubov called the world of the plays, and his article as well, "The Dark Kingdom," by which he meant primarily the business world of Moscow with its lack of enlightenment and patriarchal abuse of authority. To describe the domestic and business petty tyranny typical of "the dark kingdom" Dobroliubov used the word *samodurstvo*.

Ostrovsky himself had used the word for such abuse in the play *V chuzhom piru pokhmel'e* (Drunk at a Foreign Feast, 1856). The wealthy businessman father of the hero is said to be a *samodur* or tyrant at home; he ruins the lives of his family for no reason but to exercise his authority. As one speaker informs another about the son:

> There's no joy in his home. His father is such a savage, authoritarian man with a rugged heart.
> What do you mean: a rugged heart?
> *Samodur.*
> *Samodur!* What the devil is that! . . .

The first speaker must then explain this term of popular speech to the second:

> A *samodur*—that's when a person won't listen to anyone. You can hammer it into his head, and he'll still have his way. He'll tap his foot, and say: 'Do you know who I am?' Then everyone in the house must fall prostrate before him, or take the consequences." (Act I, Sc. 1; II, 10)

Ostrovsky's *samodur* exceeds in tyranny the familiar stock character of the commedia dell'arte or Molière's plays, who is sure to be vanquished by reason and young love in the end. For Ostrovsky's is a later age of Realism in which negative forces often enough prevail. The *samodur* in *Drunk at a Foreign Feast* not only imposes the bride of his choice on his son, but even dooms him to ignorance by forbidding him to study. The other son has been reduced to simple-mindedness since childhood by a blow on the head. Beside ignorance, superstition is rife in the household.

Of course, domestic tyranny had appeared in Ostrovsky's plays before it was given a name in *Drunk at a Foreign Feast*. The business man Bolshov in *A Family Affair* exercised it, and its first full-blown representative was a woman and an aristocrat, the cruel guardian in *Vospitannitsa* (The Ward, 1855). Indeed, Dobrolyubov inveighs especially against the tyrannical matriarch in the plays of Ostrovsky's first decade. Whether man or woman, businessman, aristocrat, or civil servant, the *samodur* demands that the young submit in the name of respect, even if the norms of the old order he represents are as distorted as those of *A Profitable Post*. Inevitably the *samodur* has the weight of authority on his side, as parent, guardian, or employer; or else he wields the power of wealth, like the rich brother in *Poverty's No Vice.*

Women are more often the victims of *samodurstvo* than men. The son's subjugation in *Drunk at a Foreign Feast* would have been easier had he been a daughter. "What are daughters!" his mother says. "You can lock them up, and you have fewer worries with them—you don't need to teach them anything" (Act II, Sc. 2; II, 26). Even when daughters do receive an education, it consists only in the empty preparation for marriage given to the poor bride and the two marriageable girls of *A Profitable Post.* The jealous guardian-ship over girls makes marriage a liberation for them, as for the two Kukushkina girls, or the two girls subject to the *samodurstvo* of their brothers in the third Balzaminov play. One of the latter declares: "Men are, in general, more fortunate than women," adding: "Woman's misfortune lies in her being always under some authority or other" (Tableau 2, Sc. 5; II, 368). One mother, repre-sentative of that authority in the first Balzaminov play, deprecates women quite as much as the mother in *Drunk at a Foreign Feast:* "What's a woman after all! What is she good for! A hen's not a bird, a woman's not a human being!" (Tableau 3, Sc. 3; II, 135). Polina Kukushkina deprecates herself and her sister to Zhadov: "We're altogether uneducated after all. Yulinka knows a thing or two, but I'm altogether an idiot . . . I don't know anything, haven't read anything, and don't understand anything of what you talk about sometimes, absolutely not a thing!" (Act II, Sc. 7; II, 68). Almost as illiterate as serfs, the women subject to *samodurstvo* will not be liberated along with them in 1861.

Those who seek liberation in marriage find it, more often than not, a second subjugation. One of them—Katherine in *Groza* (The Storm, 1860)—will escape the *samodurstvo* of a loveless marriage in death. Dobrolyubov hailed Katherine's suicide as a protest, and followed his first article with a second, "A Ray of Light in the Dark Kingdom" (1860).

III *The Height of* The Storm: *"A Ray of Light in the Dark Kingdom"* (1860)

The heroine Katherine in *The Storm,* married to a man she does not love, finds herself in the power of the worst *samodur* in the Ostrovsky canon, her mother-in-law, Kabanikha. Her husband, Tikhon, escapes his mother on a business trip, but refuses to take

Katherine along for fear she might hinder the drinking spree he plans while away. Tikhon's sister Varvara—still unmarried and thus free to keep company with her friend Kudryash—steals a key so that Katherine and she can both go out to meet their friends. For Katherine has fallen in love for the first time with Boris before she has ever even spoken to him. They become lovers, but Katherine's sense of guilt, intensified by a thunderstorm, impels her to confess her sin to her husband, and, incidentally, to many others who have taken shelter from the storm. Boris, who must obey his *samodur* uncle Dikoy, is sent away as punishment. Varvara and Kudryash go away together. Katherine, unable alone to face the now justified malevolence of Kabanikha and the townspeople, throws herself to her death in the Volga.

For the first time in an Ostrovsky play, the natural setting and the small-town environment play an essential part in the action. Set in the fictitious town of Kalinov on the Volga, all the scenes except one occur outdoors, and at least three make the natural setting accessory to the action. The time of day and the season, so much more perceptible outdoors than in, also play a part. The "drama," as Ostrovsky calls this play in distinction to his earlier comedies, takes place in summer. Acts I and V are set in the town park on a high bank overlooking the Volga river and the fields beyond. In these town scenes—and in Act IV, set in a frescoed gallery which also affords a view of the river—townspeople both speak singly and act as a chorus. The turning point of the second scene of Act II is romantically set in a ravine at night, and the last act also exploits darkness.

Music enhances the play's effect, for the character Kuligin sings, and so does Kudryash, accompanying himself on the guitar. Literally, of course, a drama with music is a "melodrama," a play which in the pejorative sense exploits a sense of dread. Certainly *The Storm* melodramatically exploits thunderclaps to heighten emotional tension at several points. In particular, the breaking of the storm at the end of Act IV forces the action to its climax.

Not only the river as an element of nature, but also the mores of a river town, on which Ostrovsky gathered material during his 1856 trip for the Marine Ministry, are essential to this play. Both river and town embody elements of good and evil: the river with its panorama inviting to distance and freedom, yet with its threatening storm; the town with the gifted, forward-looking craftsman Kuligin and the irrepressible young lovers Varvara and Kudryash, yet also with the monstrous Kabanikha and Dikoy, and its general *samodurstvo,* of which Kuligin says: "Customs are cruel in our town, sir, cruel!" (Act I, Sc. 3; II, 214). Kudryash says something similar: "You know the way people are here. They'll eat you up, put the nails in your coffin" (Act III, Tableau 2, Sc. 2; II, 244). Clearly Kalinov represents Dobrolyubov's "dark kingdom," and its society is divided as he envisaged it into the rich versus the poor, the old versus the young, those in authority versus the disenfranchised. Ostrovsky had read with approval Dobrolyubov's discussion of "the dark kingdom," and this undoubtedly led him to intensify further his picture of it. [6]

Whether Dobrolyubov so accurately understood the essence of *The Storm* in his second article, "A Ray of Light in the Dark Kingdom," is questionable. The philosopher and critic Dmitry Pisarev was more likely right when he contended in 1864 that Katherine's end could hardly be considered a conscious protest against *samodurstvo:* "Education and life could not give Katherine either firmness of character or intellectual development." Only "intelligent and cultivated people" can be "rays" of light who "consciously" change life to "better conditions of existence." [7] Indeed Katherine has a lyric and emotional nature, not a rational one.

Katherine had spent her youth in a small town similar to Kalinov in which, though, she had known idyllic happiness and beautiful religious experience. She still feels the impulse to freedom: "Why don't people fly?" she asks (Act I, Sc. 7; II, 221). She dreams of sailing down the Volga with music. Thus from early on the river connotes freedom for Katherine.

In her marriage to a husband she does not love, she experiences only a lack of freedom. Since Tikhon refuses to take her on his travels, she can learn of the world only from the pilgrim Feklusha's wild tales of unnatural natural history. "Bitter is lack of freedom, oh! how bitter! Who would not weep from it! And worst of all, we women!" (Act II, Sc. 10; II, 235). Her religious orientation shifts from the elan of salvation to fear of damnation, so that the confused threats of a mad gentlewoman of the town terrify her: "What are you doing, pretty girls," the madwoman says to Katherine and Varya. "Waiting for a date, waiting for your beaux? . . . Happy in your beauty? Look where beauty gets you (pointing to the Volga). Down there, to the very bottom . . ." (Act I, Sc. 8; II, 223). The frescoes of hell in the gallery and the breaking of the storm intensify Katherine's consciousness of sin.

Her sense of guilt is, however, not reasoned, and her suicide is not rationally planned. Indeed, Katherine seems incapable of carrying out a conscious plan. For instance, she makes her public confession on impulse, and is generally as subject to impulse and indecision as a Dostoevskian character. After publicly repenting her sin, she still thinks she can find happiness if Boris takes her away with him.

Surprisingly, the Soviet critic Yury Osnos counts Boris, that other victim of oppression, among the play's near villains. Osnos finds him all too stiff and passive, the mere "object" of Katherine's "unassuaged thirst for love."[8] True, Boris does leave her to pay for the sin to which both have been a party; he even refers to her in her presence in the third person, as if it were already all over with her: "Only one thing one must ask of God, that she may die quickly, that she need not suffer long! Farewell!" (Act V, Sc. 3; II, 263). Perhaps, though, he should be viewed not as a person but merely as a cog in the wheel of the play's mechanism, the "outsider," who later, in the Naturalistic drama of Henrik Ibsen and Gerhart Hauptmann, served to facilitate the exposition and then precipitate the action to its close.

The formal elements of *The Storm* aroused the approbation of Ostrovsky's contemporary, the novelist Ivan Goncharov, who evaluated the play for the Academy of Sciences as part of the process leading to its recognition by an Uvarov Prize in 1860. Goncharov thought the play unprecedented in Russian drama because, whether "by its plan of structure, its dramatic movement, or finally, its characters—everywhere it reveals strength of creativity, subtlety of observation and elegance of execution."[9]

Of all the critical reactions to *The Storm*, doubtless Apollon Grigorev's was the most perceptive. In his articles "After Ostrovsky's *Storm*: Letters to Ivan Sergeevich Turgenev" (1860), Grigorev found Dobrolyubov's concept of *samodurstvo* lacking in human appreciation. The father in *Drunk at a Foreign Feast*, the first character in Ostrovsky's work to be called a *samodur*, exhibits deeper charm and interest than if he were nothing but a *samodur*, Grigorev maintains. For he is the creation of "a poet and not a satirist, just as the creator of Falstaff was not a satirist."[10]

From this Grigorev concludes: "To express the meaning of all these . . . human relationships depicted by an artist with depth and sympathy, the word '*samodurstovo*' is too narrow, and the name of a satirist exposing evil, of a critic of abuses is altogether unsuited to a poet who plays on all the notes and all the keys of ordinary people's lives. . . . Such a writer, great with all his faults, must be called not a satirist, but a poet of the people [narodnyi poet]."[11] Grigorev's view of *The Storm* thus emphasized not so much the protest implicit in Katherine's death as the poetry of her passion, and the sweep of Russian life as depicted in the play. In this interpretation Ostrovsky's play is more than an exposure of social abuse: it is, above all, a human drama.

Since its first performance in 1859, the year before its publication, *The Storm* has remained a major classic of the Russian stage, and directors and actresses have offered ever new interpretations of Katherine. For example, the nineteenth-century actress Maria Ermolova evidently combined poetry and protest in the role, whereas one of the greatest Katherines, Polina Strepetova, brought out her religious mysticism and passion. The twentieth-century director Vsevolod Meyerhold and his designer Alexander Golovin strove to render the poetic atmosphere of the lovers' rendezvous, which Grigorev had singled out as the play's most important moment: "That unprecedented night of meeting in the ravine, all emanating proximity to the Volga, all breathing the smell of grass on its broad meadows, all resonant with gay singing, merry and secret talk, all full of the magic both of cheerful, uninhibited passion and of tragically fateful passion "[12]

The Czech composer Leoš Janáček in his opera of 1921, *Katya Kabanova*, based upon *The Storm*, changed some characters slightly but not altogether felicitously. He gave Kudryash traits from Kuligin and dropped the latter's near-raisonneur role; he had Kabanikha and Dikoy join in a scene of illicit sensuality and drunkenness together. The Soviet critic Shtein, who insists that the play takes in more than just its heroine's fate, objected to Janáček's naming his opera for her alone, and also criticized the opera's basic line of recitative, which leaves unused the songs already present in the text of the play.

While Janáček wrote his opera 100 years after Ostrovsky's birth, the avant-garde Moscow Taganka Theater marked the playwright's one-hundred-fiftieth anniversary with a dramatic "composition" featuring *The Storm*. So this major play continues to inspire stage productions and stimulate further creative effort.

IV   *X-Ray of Light:* Sin and Sorrow Are Common to All *(1863)*

Soon after *The Storm* Ostrovsky again dealt with the theme of a faithless wife in *Grekh da beda na kogo ne zhivet* (*Sin and Sorrow Are Common to All*), published in January of 1863, in Dostoevsky's journal *Vremya*.

The young estate owner Babaev, while on a business trip to a provincial capital, seeks distraction for the four days of his stay with Tanya, who, though a poor girl, was brought up with him. Economic necessity has meanwhile forced Tanya to marry a shopkeeper, Krasnov, who has quarreled with his own family because he does not demand of her the work usual in his class. In this instance, though, he reverts to the authoritarian attitudes of the lower class and forbids her to see Babaev again, or at best only once more. The nobleman suggests regular secret rendezvous at an apartment he will rent on future visits. Though Tanya tries, on the advice of her conniving sister Zhmigulina, to deceive Krasnov, she is denounced both by Afon, her husband's crippled brother, and his sister Kuritsyna, who see her with Babaev. Throwing off deceit, she requests a separation from her husband. He thereupon kills her and gives himself up to justice.

At first glance *Sin and Sorrow Are Common to All* seems at every important turn to reverse the action of *The Storm*: it weaves together planned adultery, conscious deceit, and a crime of passion. But in fact the play is no antithesis of the earlier one, but rather gives a different perspective on the marriage of convenience.

True, Katherine's conduct could cause the same reaction as Tanya's. An undercurrent of disapproval at the heroine's immorality was present in the enthusiasm with which *The Storm* was received at its St. Petersburg opening in 1859; Apollon Grigorev reported: "With the burst of enthusiasm which greeted the daring scene of the rendezvous in *The Storm*—with the general Russian sentiment for the poetic truth of this scene—a hostile hissing of disapproval made itself heard from the boxes and various orchestra rows, which became almost a noticeable, even distinct howl at the immorality of the play."[13] Yet Ostrovsky presents Katherine not as adulterous, but as true to her name, which means in Greek "eternally pure." Whether because she tries to be true to a husband not of her own choice, or because it is she herself who discloses the guilt no one suspects, or because she chooses to die for her first and only love, she emerges as more sinned against than sinning. Tanya, however, is very different, for she tries to have it both ways: to love as she will, and yet to maintain the outward form of a marriage which she has not allowed to be consummated, because it was contracted under duress of poverty. Dmitry Pisarev rightly called her "a very shabby little woman," who did not even deserve the wrath of her husband, that "Russian Othello,"[14] as Pisarev ironically called him. The background of nature is not exploited in this play as it was in *The Storm*, though its nominal location on the river made it one of the general series Ostrovsky planned as "Nights on the Volga." Nor was the execution of the erring wife by her wronged husband a response to the reaction to *The Storm*'s "immorality," as if Ostrovsky had shown the adulteress drastically punished upon audience demand. For the basic difference between the two plays lies in a distinction made by Apollon Grigorev (though he was speaking of Tolstoy, not Ostrovsky): "How many frogs blow themselves up . . . into oxen, . . . how many people want to seem criminal to themselves and others, when they have committed only a small meanness [*poshlost'*]."[15] The people in *Sin and Sorrow Are Common to All*—with the possible exception of the husband—are frogs in Grigorev's sense.

Certainly "small meanness" is the essence of Babaev's character. Grigorev faulted Katherine's lover Boris for "lack of definition [*bezlichnost'*]",[16] but Babaev is even worse. He is a liar when he pretends to have come purposely to see Tanya; actually he heard only after arriving in town on a business trip that she lived there. Far from loving her, he sees her as another conquest to be added to his "collection," like Merich's in *A Poor Bride*. Though he swears to respect her chastity upon her insistence, he has no intention of keeping his word.

If we grant that Tanya may love Babaev at the start, thanks to recollections of their childhood friendship, it is hard to understand how she can continue to do so. For example, he did not carry out his mother's wish that Tanya, the daughter of the family's clerk, be allowed to stay on at the estate: "Where were you," Tanya asks him, "when we had nothing to eat!" (Act II, Tableau 2, Sc. 3; II, 421). She realizes, too, that his selfish urging puts her in a difficult predicament. "You don't love me the least bit," she says, aware that his insistence on future secret meetings takes no account of the danger to her: ". . . he [her husband] will find me out down to the bottom of the sea" (Act II, Tableau 2, Sc. 4; II, 422). She admits that she has only herself to blame for her present plight: "I myself married him," she says of her husband, "no one compelled me" (Act IV, Tableau 1, Sc. 3; II, 442). And yet, fully recognizing both the difficulties of her plight and Babaev's inadequacies, she still entrusts herself to him.

Tanya's awareness shows her to be anything but simple-minded, a quality which Babaev counts a good reason for loving her. If she were more naive, her character might have some of the poetry of Katherine's. Instead Tanya is weak and self-seeking in wanting to remain within the limits of formal morality and at the same time to play at loving another man. Apparently she does not actually sin with Babaev, thanks to the improbable limits of time and place on their, meetings (once in the public park, and twice for very brief times). She has, nevertheless, cheated her husband by marrying him and then remaining beyond his reach, by consenting to deceive him, and by finally confessing her deceit only when she must. Still, even if she is "an empty, fickle-minded woman,"[17] as a contemporary critic termed her, she has not deserved death. Nor is morality at issue in the play.

Rather the play reflects old versus new views of marriage and of morality for women, and lower- versus upper-class modes of conduct. According to the dictates of the sixteenth-century Domostroy, a compilation of practical moral precepts which provided the norm for Krasnov's lower class, he has the right to judge her: "I am her husband, I am also her judge" (Act IV, Tableau 2, Sc. 6; II, 447). Such an attitude, which had become reactionary by the nineteenth century, contradicts, though, his own defense of the modern, enlightened relationship he had established with his wife previously.

All this makes his drastic execution of his wife very implausible, and yet Krasnov's act was based upon an actual occurrence. Indeed, it leaves the impression of a strange event in a newspaper account, and not of a widespread condition against which steps should be taken. Grigorev wrote of the earlier plays in his article "Art and Morality" (1861): "The mire is to blame [Tina vinovata],"[18] and by mire he meant "views of life, honor, love, and woman which are disgraceful to human feeling."[19] The "protest" of The Storm then, as Grigorev said in the same article, cried out "for a new basis of people's lives, for freedom of the mind, the will and the feeling."[20] Sin and Sorrow Are Common to All has no such general meaning, and no ray of light emanates from two-timing Tanya's fate. Nor did the award of an Uvarov Prize to Sin and Sorrow make it the equal of The Storm.

Evidently actors viewed the range of passion experienced by the husband—from joy on returning home to a wife he believes loves him as he loves her, through jealous rage, the passion of murder, and final resignation—as a challenge. The play held sufficient interest to place it among the ten Ostrovsky plays most often staged during his lifetime. It has lost its audience appeal since then, however.

CHAPTER 4

Beyond the Familiar Frame: Historical Plays and a Folklore Myth

I *The National Past:* A Dream on the Volga *(1865)*

IN the 1840s, as Lidia Lotman points out,[1] Ostrovsky and his young progressive friends had complained over the fact that the meretricious glorification of the past and of the monarchy had not been driven from the stage by a more truthful and Realistic view of history. Over the ensuing years the fictions of the reactionaries were disproved by history itself: the death of Nicholas I, which marked the end of an era; Russia's defeat in the Crimean War; the emancipation of the serfs by Alexander II. Now historical plays were written quite different from the earlier *okhranitel'nye* (imperial-conservative) historical dramas, as the young Turgenev had called them.[2] Such plays exposing tyranny were *The Czar's Bride* (1849) and *The Girl from Pskov* (1859) by Lev Mey, both of which Nikolay Rimsky-Korsakov transformed into operas. After 1865 Ostrovsky's friend Aleksey Pisemsky wrote three plays on topics from Russian history of the eighteenth century. Then Aleksey Konstantinovich Tolstoy launched his trilogy on the time of Ivan the Terrible (1866, 1868, 1870), which did not decry so much tyranny as quite factually present the problems faced by ruler and people.

Ostrovsky joined the painters of historical canvases with his so-called "chronicle play," *Koz'ma Zakhar'ich Minin, Sukhoruk* (Kozma Zakharich Minin, the One-Armed, 1862), which showed the people's leader Kozma Minin gathering a resistance force against the invading Poles at the beginning of the seventeenth century. The fact that the play was named for the resistance leader caused the censorship to call it "democratic." As Ostrovsky ironically commented in a letter of 1862 to Apollon Grigorev: "he [Minin] collected money for a great cause. . . . If Minin is a democrat, then so is Mikhail Romanov [a nobleman member of the resistance who then became the first of the imperial dynasty which ruled Russia for the next three hundred years]. . . ."[3] Beginning with *Voevoda* (The War Lord [1865], subtitled Dream on the Volga), Ostrovsky wrote three historical plays in succession, one a year, and then two in later years, making with *Minin* a total of six in ten years.

Roman Dubrovin, the hero of *Dream on the Volga*, a river-pirate Robin Hood of the seventeenth century, has gathered a band of outlaws who have been unjustly dispossessed like himself by the war lord and governor Shalygin. The tyrannical ruler has carried off not only Dubrovin's wife, Olena, but also the young nobleman Bastryukov's fiancée, Maria Vlasevna. The outlaws plan to rescue the two women during the war lord's absence. Warned by a dream, Shalygin intervenes at the moment of the rescue, but a second intervention by a new governor sent to replace Shalygin gives victory to the rescuers.

Commenting on Ostrovsky's historical plays in the recent edition of his complete works, Lidia Lotman emphasizes the importance both of Ostrovsky's archival research on the Volga region, and of his personal impressions gained by observation beginning in the 1840s. She finds: "The tragic scene of Shalygin pursuing Maria Vlasevna in the passages of the war lord's mansion was obviously up to a point inspired in the author by his impressions of the architecture of the historic Volga houses."[4]

Both *Minin* and *Dream on the Volga* were to be included in the series "Nights on the Volga," conceived the year after Ostrovsky's 1856 expedition to the Volga. Certainly both show in their archaic and folk language the results of the linguistic observations he made there. More than *Minin* in prose, though, the verse play *Dream on the Volga* reflects the poetry of songs and tales which Ostrovsky absorbed in the river towns. Above all, the play's very subject is drawn from the folk ballad "Stenka Razin" about the river-pirate hero and his band, who launched the most important people's rebellion of the seventeenth century. True, Razin is actually mentioned only once, when one of Dubrovin's men announces, after the successful conclusion of their undertaking, that he will now join the historic hero.

Lotman adds the parallel of Dubrovin's band, like Razin's, protesting their leader's involvement with a woman: Shcherbak (Dubrovin's second in command):

What kind of cause is this? A woman is it?
Then better give it up. Who's tied to them
Is himself a woman. (Act II, Tableau 2, Sc. 3; VI, 185)

While underlining the revolutionary character of Dubrovin and
Razin's cause, Lotman also brings out the folklore traits of the
resemblance between them. Shalygin's magician Mizgir also springs
from folk tradition, as do the folk songs, some accompanied on the
gusli, or zither. Lotman buttresses N. P. Kashin's claim that the folk
songs and ballads Ostrovsky heard on the 1856 trip supplied the
core of his inspiration for *Dream on the Volga.* [5]

The dream of the title itself belongs to the folk beliefs in the play.
Such beliefs, as well as fairy tales of the Russian people, were being
collected at this time by Alexander Afanasiev, who was also a staff
member of *Sovremennik,* and of whose work Ostrovsky was surely
aware.

More important than the material included in the play is the
dramatic use Ostrovsky made of it. Like *The Storm,* this play utilizes
the sweep of the river to denote the freedom of nature in contrast to
the women's confinement in chambers. And the picturesque enters
with a vengeance in the second tableau of Act II (VI, 179):

A wooded gorge; at the left a hill, in it a cave; beyond the hill a ravine and
stream which winds into the distance upstage; beyond the stream a hill, on
it the walls of a monastery are visible through the forest; a bridge across the
river; on the right a wooded hill, along it a road leads to the bridge, and
then ascends to the monastery; on the hillside bushes and a hut.

Dream on the Volga presents an even broader spectrum of people
than *The Storm.* Thus the stage directions just cited continue:
"Beggars on the bridge. A hermit is coming with a pail from the
stream. Pilgrims in prayer are crossing the bridge to the monastery"
(VI, 179). The spread of social classes reaches from the nobleman
Bastryukov to a peasant woman singing a lullaby, from the outlaw
members of Dubrovin's band, including wandering players
[*skomorokhi*], to Shalygin's soldiers. Dubrovin himself and his
immediate associates represent the middle class and craftsmen. Not
all these people have a direct function in the plot. The hermit, for
example, like Dosuzhev in *A Profitable Post,* serves as a discussion
partner in contrast to the activist Dubrovin; the hermit, who has
also suffered wrongs, preferred to withdraw from the world rather
than seek to set it right. When the hermit warns against committing

unjust acts to achieve justice, Dubrovin raises his hands to Heaven like William Tell, and insists they are not bloody.[6] The multitude provides more than a foil to the principal protagonists, however. After Pushkin's example in *Boris Godunov*, Ostrovsky has made the people the true hero of his play. The peasant woman who sings a lullaby is one of its spokesmen; her song, incidentally, is an authentic folk song, "collected" with both melody and words from oral tradition by Ostrovsky on the Volga expedition:

Refrain: Lullaby, sweet little grandson,
  Sleep, sleep, you son of peasants.
Stanza 2: God has forgotten us, the tsar's without money,
  People have thrown us out, handed us over to people;
  We must live on our own, work for a living,
  In the great world please masters.
  (Act IV, Sc. 3; VI, 209–10)

The attitude of the song, which resembles that of George Gershwin's "I got plenty o' nuttin' " from *Porgy and Bess*, is emphasized when the old woman replies cynically to the boatman's question about her feudal lord: "One Tartar's like another" (Act IV, Sc. 1; VI, 204). The same cynical pessimism about the people's rulers infects the standard hope that with a new ruler a new era has dawned; again, as at the end of *The Poor Bride*, anonymous voices resound:

Old businessmen: "Well, the old one's bad, just as the new one'll be."
Young businessmen: "Yes, he's got to be the same, if not worse."
  (Act V, Sc. 6; VI, 240)

Unlike the peasant woman, Olena and Maria Vlasevna oppose the war lord, who seizes them like booty. They practice passive resistance against his advances and act as spies for the rescue effort, though a spy of their own sex is, in turn, assigned to them. Maria Vlasevna displays unexpected agility in running away from Shalygin through the wilderness of a garden; moreover, she staunchly speaks for herself both at the start and also at the end, when she appears before the new ruler. He asks:

  In the edict there is nothing about the girl.
  Whose bride is she—. . . We'll ask her parents.
Bastryukov: Ask her.

Ruler: Does a girl know
                     Who her bridegroom is? Should she decide?
                     Whom will you marry?
Maria: Stephan Bastryukov. (Act V, Sc. 5; VI, 234)

In whatever century, then, Ostrovsky's women will dispose of themselves, and not be disposed of like property.

The play's main political thrust—liberation from an unjust ruler—is, however, relegated to a dream. To cleanse himself of sin before his marriage to Maria Vlasevna, the war lord makes a pilgrimage. While spending a night at the hut where the old woman is singing her lullaby, he dreams of his bloody deeds, of standing trial for them, even of being caught and drowned by Dubrovin. Was a dream of liberation as far as the playwright dared go, if his play were to pass the censor?

Though Ostrovsky had many censorship difficulties in this decade, he had none with this play. Moreover, despite the difficulties it presents to production, it was among his ten most often staged plays during his lifetime, although it has since almost disappeared from the repertory. Anton Arensky's operatic version, *Dream on the Volga* (1890), is now better known than the original play.

II   *A Russian Fairy Tale:* The Snow Maiden *(1873)*

It seems truly miraculous that the Realist Ostrovsky, famous for a quarter century for his depictions of contemporary life, should in mid-career write a fairy-tale drama in verse which stands alone in his canon. In a perceptive chapter on *Snegurochka* (The Snow Maiden, 1873), Abram Shtein tells how Savva Mamontov, the opera Maecenas, asked Ostrovsky: "Where did you find the characters and the poetry of *The Snow Maiden*?" To that the author replied, citing the same source Pushkin used for his fairy tales: "Why, my nanny told them all to me."[7] Though no tale specifically of this content is to be found in Alexander Afanasiev's *Fairy Tales of the Russian People* (1855–64), the Russian collection comparable to that of the Brothers Grimm, Shtein claims that every Russian child knows a folk tale about a snow maiden: a childless couple, Ivan and Maria, make a snow maiden, who to their delight comes to life as their thirteen-year-old daughter. Unfortunately, though, while playing with other children she jumps over a bonfire and melts. From this folk subject, then, Ostrovsky fashioned a verse drama in a prologue and four acts with its pageant of greeting the spring enacted by a prehistoric people, the Berendeans. In his play a universal and a personal mystery come alive: the return of the light and spring after the darkness of winter, and the mystery of life and death; in its individual psychological meaning, the play also deals with the gain and loss inherent in love.

Snow Maiden, the daughter of Spring and Grandfather 'Frost (Ded Moroz; perhaps better, the Snow King), is placed in the care of the landless peasants Bobyl and Bobylinkha as foster parents. The money-minded couple make the shepherd Lel pay to stay the night, though he asks only a flower in return for singing his songs to Snow Maiden. Mizgir, a wealthy young businessman, is engaged to the village girl Kupava but leaves her upon falling in love at first sight with Snow Maiden. Kupava brings her case before the Emperor Berendey; but Mizgir defends himself by exhibiting Snow Maiden's beauty, though he does complain of her coldness. The emperor sets both Mizgir and Lel the task of competing for her love. Snow Maiden prefers Lel, but he prefers Kupava. Snow Maiden appeals to her mother for a loving heart. Spring grants her request, while warning her that it may mean her end. She does then melt in the embrace of Mizgir, who in despair throws himself into the lake. Nevertheless the Berendeans celebrate the festival of greeting the sun god Yarilo, at which all engaged couples are to marry.

The play impresses one by its feeling for nature above all. The magic of winter's icy shapes in moonlight glistens through Frost's gleeful song in the Prologue:

> I resolve to have fun, take my club,
> Brighten, silver the night,
> With my usual sweep and expanse.
> Around the rich mansions
> Rap at the corners,
> Squeak at the gate posts,
> Sing 'neath sleigh runners,
> Have my fun,
> Fun, fun, fun. (Prologue, Sc. 2; VII, 369)

Juxtaposed with this at the play's end is the song of a chorus of birds, Spring's retinue; and finally the Berendeans chant a welcome to the white-clad youth Yarilo, who arrives in a procession of plenty for the festival banquet:

Light and strength,
Young Sun god.
Refrain: Our red sun!
None is more beautiful
In all the world:
Give us, god of light,
A warm summer. (Act IV, Sc. 4; VII 456–57)

Together with a deep feeling for nature, the play reflects an increasing interest in folklore at that time. Afanasiev had not only made the definitive collection of Russian fairy tales, but had also followed it with *Poeticheskie vozzreniia slavian na prirodu* (Poetic Views of Nature as Seen by the Slavic Peoples, 1866–69). This work of Afanasiev must have led Ostrovsky to include Lel, the figure in Slavic mythology corresponding to Pan or Eros of the Greek myths. In her notes to *The Snow Maiden,* Lotman identifies the observances of the sun festival as those of the summer solstice on St. Peter's Day, June 29, about which Ostrovsky consulted historians, though in his play he moved the festival to April. Shtein remarks that the flower which wakes the Snow Maiden to love is Love-in-idleness, used to like purpose in Shakespeare's *Midsummer Night's Dream* (Act II, Sc. 1).

Indeed, the play may contain quite as many themes from literature as from folk custom. Thus, one major theme is Snow Maiden's plea to her mother for a human heart: "Though I die, I hold one moment of love / Dearer than years of grief and tears" (Act IV, Sc. 2; VII, 449). The heroine Undine makes the same sacrifice in Friedrich de la Motte Fouqué's fairy tale and Jean Giraudoux' play; Hans Christian Andersen's little mermaid undergoes something similar; and the dyer's wife in Hugo von Hofmannsthal's *Woman without a Shadow* prefers a mortal's pain to the eternal bliss of her immortal nature.

A broad spectrum of humanity is represented by the Berendeans, historically a Turkish tribe whom Ostrovsky transforms into a prehistoric Slavic people. At the low end of the scale are the ignoble step-parents Bobyl and Bobylikha, who try to make Snow Maiden lure lovers for pay. High on the scale stands the noble, genial Emperor Berendey, who is something of a troubadour king like Good King René of Anjou, and also of a Slavic father figure, like Tsar Saltan in Pushkin's fairy tale of that name. Berendey refuses to issue a repressive decree, suggested by his incompetent prime minister

Bermyata, which would compel faithfulness in wives. Instead he prefers positive action to further the cause of love and beauty. He is concerned for his people because

> In their hearts I have seen a coldness. . .
> Nor do they serve beauty any more.
>
> (Act II, Sc. 2; VII, 413)

The humans Mizgir and Kupava are quite as stereotyped as their partners in love, the demigods Snow Maiden and Lel. Though their passion provides the motor of the action, it is less psychological than metaphysical.

The play was intended for folk festivals, and in its ritual the seeming commonplace of renewal in nature has simple, profound significance. Above all, there is poetry in its songs, written in a shorter line than the blank verse of the play as a whole. Some of the twenty-three songs are original with Ostrovsky; some he adapted from earlier tradition: thus the *gusli* players' song in Berendey's palace draws heavily upon the rhythm and diction of the national epic, "The Lay of Prince Igor."

The Snow Maiden took Ostrovsky's contemporaries by surprise. His longtime editor Nekrasov thought it inferior and would not pay the usual fee for it, so that Ostrovsky published it elsewhere, in *Vestnik Evropy* (The Messenger of Europe). The young composer Peter Tschaikovsky, though, was charmed by *The Snow Maiden*, for which he was commissioned to write stage music. Almost a decade later the artist Viktor Vasnetsov of "The World of Art" group designed imaginative sets for Savva Mamontov's production (1881) at his epoch-making theater near Moscow.

Another composer, Nikolay Rimsky-Korsakov, composed an opera to the libretto he himself made from its plot, and again Vasnetsov did the designs for the Mamontov production of the opera (1885). Unfortunately Rimsky's opera—which deletes certain poetic passages, including Frost's song—is much better known than the play; indeed, in the West it is the only known form of Ostrovsky's *Snow Maiden*. The Metropolitan Opera version of 1923, in French with an English translation from the French, even used the Russian title in French transliteration, *Snégourotchka*.

Through these several mediations *The Snow Maiden* continued to catch the imagination of artists and musicians, if not of the general public. Valentin Serov made several pictures on its themes; Boris

Kustodiev designed sets for a Bolshoy Opera production of 1918;
and Nicholas Roerich designed the productions of both the Russian
Theater (St. Petersburg, 1912) and the Chicago Opera (1929). Two
different ballets have been choreographed, both based on
Tschaikovsky's music.

A feminist-oriented audience must find extreme both the Eros
motif of the woman's need of a male in order to come to life and the
doglike submission which at least Kupava promises in return. But
modern audiences must also approve of the importance the play
assigns to love and free choice in marriage. In any case, this play's
dream of a bright realm of art and carefree love in the forest
primeval became part of the burst of fantasy and color with which
Russian opera, ballet, and music astonished the world in the Paris
seasons just before World War I.

CHAPTER 5

The Practiced Professional on Themes of a New Age

I *Careerist at Any Cost:* The Diary of a Scoundrel (*1868*)

AFTER almost two decades as a successful playwright, and two Uvarov Prizes—one for a truly great play, *The Storm*— Ostrovsky began to be reproached with having exhausted his creativity. Paradoxically it was Ivan Goncharov, who had recommended him for one prize, who now, in an unfinished article defending him against that reproach, raised a more serious charge against him. Fortunately Goncharov's piece, written about 1874, was published only in 1924. All in refuting the accusation that the playwright had exhausted his forces, Goncharov explains the disappearance of the old Ostrovsky by the vanishing, after the Emancipation, of the world he had been used to depicting, as if the playwright had portrayed only the one world for which he was famous. "He has nothing ahead of him," Goncharov maintains; "the new Russia is not his thing."[1] Certainly so narrow a conception of Ostrovsky as solely the dramatist of "the dark kingdom" cannot stand against the play literally entitled *Na vsiakogo mudretsa dovol'no prostoty*, (Even a Wiseman Stumbles, 1868), or, as it is better known in English, *The Diary of a Scoundrel*[2] The play is a breath of fresh air, with its wit and brittle satire on the high society of the new era.

The scoundrel of the English title, Glumov, determined to rise in the world by all necessary means, insinuates himself into his uncle Mamaev's good graces by defaming another nephew, the young hussar Kurchaev. Mamaev so favors Glumov that he even asks him to pay court to his wife, a society coquette who needs suitors as a plant needs rain. Mamaev also introduces him to Gorodulin, for whom Glumov writes a liberal speech, and to General Krutitsky, for whom Glumov ghost-writes a conservative tract. Mamaev finally presents Glumov as the virtuous fiancé the rich bourgeois widow

Turusina seeks for her richly dowered niece Mashenka. Now Mashenka must marry him or lose her fortune, though she and Kurchaev are in love. When Mamaeva, incensed at her admirer's engagement, goes to confront him, she finds, and steals, his diary, to which he has confided his unflattering comments on his protectors. She publishes the diary, and then sends the newspaper version and the original in time to frustrate the marriage. Though Glumov is banished from society, Krutitsky foresees that he will eventually be recalled, for everyone needs him in some way.

The ending—in which Glumov confronts the assembled company—recalls the ball in Griboedov's great classic *Woe from Wit*, at which the hero Chatsky too finds himself isolated in the end, thanks to his all too witty comments on society. However, Chatsky spoke his diatribes openly, whereas Glumov has played the sycophant in public, while formulating his true opinions in a private diary. If neither Griboedov's Chatsky nor Ostrovsky's Zhadov *(A Profitable Post)* will prostitute his gifts for profit, for the careerist Glumov the ends justify any means.

Glumov has used very low means, indeed. He bribes Manefa, Turusina's fortune-teller, to use her influence in his favor; he writes anonymous letters denouncing Kurchaev; he defames that young man by showing their uncle Kurchaev's caricature of him; but above all, he prostitutes his own gifts by putting them at the service now of this, now of that opinion. As the Soviet critic Lakshin says, "he consciously and calculatedly *betrays his intelligence.*"[3]

Glumov, then, is a wise man who, with his mind for sale, still makes the one unwise mistake which causes his downfall. Lakshin generalizes on the word "wise man," proving it was used in common parlance with a quotation from Nekrasov, the editor of *Otechestvennye zapiski,* who wrote cynically of the postemancipation 1860s:

> The people haven't gained much,
> Nor do they find life easier anywhere,
> Neither thanks to the wise man official,
> Nor to fanatics of the people. . . .[4]

Nekrasov's coeditor Mikhail Saltykov-Shchedrin also termed the political sages of that time "wise men." In this sense Glumov's patrons are also wise men: Mamaev with his advice to any and all, Gorodulin with his liberal remedies, Krutitsky with his conservative wisdom. All three wise men err with respect to Glumov.

The latter betrays not only his intellect, but also his feelings. He pretends a religiosity he does not feel to Manefa and Turusina, who believes he has come as the fortune-teller had prophesied. Glumov pretends love for Mamaeva to gain her favor and that of her husband. Finally, he pretends to love Mashenka to gain her fortune. Thus the scoundrel has sold himself intellectually and emotionally in order to achieve his career goal. The first draft of the play contained a monologue in which Glumov outlined his hopes of rising in the world to the post of vice-governor. Of course, wealth would accompany position. In fact, it even comes first in his last speech: "You've deprived me of money, of reputation," he tells the society people who have ostracized him (Act V, Sc. 7; III, 79).

Indeed, money is a prime consideration for the society characters as well. Mamaeva bases her relationship with Glumov on money from the start, as she tells his mother:

If you see a handsome young man poorly dressed—that hurts, that shouldn't and shan't be, shall never be! . . . It's the rule that we must pity the poor. . . . But one's heart can hardly endure the sight of a handsome man—a young man in poverty. . . . Besides, poverty takes away that air of victory, that daring which are so pardonable, so becoming to a handsome young man." (Act II, Sc. 2; III, 24)

As for Kurchaev, too, however much it pains him to see his beloved Mashenka marry another, he hates quite as much to see her money go to his rival: "They'll give you away [in marriage] to him [Glumov]," he tells her. "They'll give away your money" (Act V, Sc. 1; III, 67). Nor does Mashenka insist on marrying her beloved if she will thereby lose her inheritance: "I am a Moscow young lady," she tells her aunt. "I shan't marry without money and the approval of my relatives. I like George Kurchaev, but if you don't, I won't marry him, nor will I waste away because of it. But have pity, dear aunt. Thanks to you, I am to have a fortune. And I want to enjoy life" (Act III, Sc. 1; III, 39).

Though all the characters, not excepting even the young couple, are part of materialistic society, Lenin found Krutitsky, played by Stanislavsky in 1918, a particularly memorable example of a budding capitalist. Lenin equated the lesson to be learned from this figure with that of an "*agitka,*"[5] or propaganda piece for Bolshevism.

Glumov is more than memorable, he is an archetype. He reappeared as a young man-about-town and mischief-maker in Ostrovsky's later play *Easy Money* (1870). Furthermore, Saltykov-Shchedrin brings the scoundrel back in the cyclical work *Sovremen-raya idilliya* (A Contemporary Idyll, 1877–1883), adapted for the stage under the title *Mr. Balalaikin* and produced by Moscow's Contemporary Theater in 1974.

In his first plan for the play Ostrovsky called his scoundrel Lazutkin [Mr. Climber], before changing his name to Glumov, which is associated with "making fun of." Like a picaresque hero of eighteenth-century fiction, Glumov exposes one milieu after another to ridicule. In this sense his progression from one to another is the thread on which successive scenes are hung. His diary, which makes fun of them all, is the dramatic device of the play's satiric exposure. Incidentally, the play is written in the standard speech of the society world with which it deals, devoid of dialect.

The existence of the diary, however essential as dramatic device, seemed improbable to some from the start. One critic wrote: "We strongly doubt that a gentleman who had resolved to make his way by sycophancy and flattery would keep diaries in which to pour out his rage and indignation at the meanness of human nature."[6] The contemporary critic Viktor Burenin thought Glumov naive to have allowed himself to be caught by means of the diary, and Alexey Suvorin charged Ostrovsky with imitating the device Gogol had used to expose his outside observer Khlestakov in *The Inspector General*.[7]

The two directors Sergey Eisenstein and Sergey Tretiakov, who produced the play while studying at Meyerhold's workshop in 1922, depicted the diary's contents in fifty feet of film, Eisenstein's first motion picture. Therewith Eisenstein began his career as a film director and abandoned the theater.

If the diary is a device, then the play has a plot, although some contemporary commentators criticized it as an unconnected succession of scenes. Indeed, the plot is artfully developed, and the play classically structured in five acts. Glumov proclaims his career aims at the start, and as with a mathematical proof pronounces the first step accomplished at the end of Act I. Act II, according to the early plan of the play, was to take place at Turusina's, whereas in the completed version it takes place at Mamaev's. Thus the second-act raveling of the plot, or *zaviazka,* begins with Mamaeva, just as does its unraveling, the denouement or *razviazka,* in Act IV: in Act II Glumov declares his love for her, while in Act IV she is incensed to learn of his engagement to Mashenka. The third act is set at the home of Turusina, who belongs to the business class, not the society world into which Glumov progresses. She holds court amid a retinue of parasite companions and the fortune-teller Manefa. The plot hinges on her decision to marry Mashenka to Glumov. That decision is based on Gorodulin's recommendation, Manefa's fake prophecy that the next person at her door will be the chosen one, and Mamaev's prompt appearance to introduce his nephew Glumov.

Almost all the acts and scenes end, if not with the bang of Glumov's heralded appearance at the close of Act III, then at least with a memorable curtain line. Thus Act I concludes with Glumov's pronouncement: "The first step [of his career plan] has been taken" (Act I, Sc. 7; III, 20). Krutitsky's concluding speech in Act IV, Scene 1, recalls Famusov's last word at the end of Act I in *Woe from Wit:* "What a chore, my heavens, to be father to a grownup daughter!" For Krutitsky is annoyed when Mamaeva darts off after wheedling from him the news of Glumov's engagement: "What has gotten into her?" he exclaims. "Heaven spare me women! They're worse than commanding a division!" (Act IV, Tableau 1, Sc. 2; III, 59).

The second scene of Act IV includes the new element usually introduced in the fourth act of a five-act classic drama to impel the action to its close: Mamaeva finds and steals Glumov's diary.

The conclusion of Act V, then, unlike the open ending of *A Poor Bride*, is as final in the comic mode as that of *The Storm* in the tragic: Glumov's diary is read aloud to the assembled company. Glumov makes the play's pointed meaning clear by wittily turning the tables on all present: "I was honest only when I wrote this diary" (Act V, Sc. 7; III, 79), he proclaims, going on to state that the diary contains nothing which they do not say about one another, only not directly. He declares that whichever of their number has stolen his diary is dishonest. Thus Glumov really has the last word by condemning his associates as scoundrels even less honest than he, and they rightly foresee his eventual recall to their midst.

Perhaps this might be considered an open ending after all, since these unpleasant characters promise no improvement, but only the same thing all over again. The play's unmitigated satire on society has proven relevant to later times as well, for *The Diary of a Scoundrel*, among the thirteen most frequently produced of Ostrovsky's plays in the half-century after his death, has since been often staged. The brilliance of its social satire links it to *A Family Affair;* but if the early play may be likened to a woodcut, then this in its sharpness is an etching.

II *A Woman's Way:* A Warm Heart *(1869)*

Though *Goriachee serdtse* (A Warm Heart) bears the date of its publication and first performance, 1869, Ostrovsky began work on it in 1868 but set it aside to write *The Diary of a Scoundrel.* It is earlier than *The Diary of a Scoundrel,* though, not only by the fact of its earlier conception, but also by its continuation of earlier concerns. Thus it is set in the preliberation period in the same merchant milieu of Kalinov, the fictive small town on the Volga, and treats in part the same theme of the oppression of a young woman as *The Storm.*

The heroine Parasha suffers the tyranny of her stepmother, Matrena, who not only deceives her husband, Kuroslepov, with his clerk Narkis, but also wields all power in the home. So the father keeps from his daughter the fortune left her by her dead mother. When Kuroslepov finds 2,000 rubles missing, the city manager Gradoboev arrests as the thief the innocent Vasya, who had crawled under a fence not to steal, but to court Parasha. Vasya is to be drafted into the army as punishment. Parasha leaves home to find and follow him, while another clerk, the faithful Gavrilo, goes with her to keep her from the dangers of the road.

A neighboring estate owner, Khlynov, is so rich that he employs Aristarch, Parasha's godfather, to devise distractions for a continuous house party. He buys Vasya off from conscription to serve as minstrel and jester for his following. His retinue, deciding to play robbers in Robin Hood style, seizes Parasha to bring her to their master. Though Aristarch saves her from any further consequences of the prank, he cannot allay her distress at finding Vasya in the role of entertainer. Matrena's paramour, Narkis, also a captive of the mock robbers, when plied with wine, boasts that he has been the beneficiary of Matrena's theft of the missing money. After Parasha is returned to her father, he restores order in his house and allows her to marry Gavrilo and receive her inheritance.

When first produced, the "lyric farce" *A Warm Heart* bore the remark: "The action takes place thirty years ago" (III, 81). According to Lakshin, this "escape clause" was added by Ostrovsky's actor friend Fedor Burdin as "a lightning rod to ward off censorship."[8]

Likewise Sergey Danilov, in his survey of nineteenth-century Russian theater, mentions another precaution against censorship: the use of *gorodnichii* for the city manager Gradoboev, a title obsolete since 1862. Danilov adds: "Despite these misleading cues, the play is steeped in a vivid sense of contemporaneity."[9] Clearly, then, the *samodurstvo* depicted in the play had to do with the postliberation period, the deceptive attributions to an earlier era notwithstanding.

Danilov accuses all three power figures in the play of *samodurstvo* and compares Parasha's rebellion against it to Katherine's protest in *The Storm*. Actually only Kuroslepov displays the true attributes of a *samodur*, and he is more ridiculous than imposing: he is hoodwinked by his wife, and so stupefied by liquor that he is either asleep or muddle-headed most of the time. For instance, the gatekeeper Silan recognizes Matrena wearing her husband's clothes in order, so disguised, to visit her lover's room. "My master has come out," Silan exclaims. "I find that very surprising because at this hour you can only get him up with a crowbar, or block and tackle, and then not successfully" (Act V, Sc. 3; III, 155). Yet when Kuroslepov sees his wife in his own overcoat and hat, he is so confused by sleep and alcohol that he tells Gradoboev: "Here I am with you, and on the threshold there I am again" (Act V, Sc. 5; III, 158).

The second near-*samodur*, Gradoboev, cloaks his *samodurstvo* with a pretense of legality and consent. Thus in Act III he emerges from his house beside the jail in gown and military cap with a pipe and crutch—accoutrements which he uses for intimidation—and addresses the populace in a famous speech:

It's high up to God, and far away to the Tsar. Am I not right?
Voices: That's right, Serapion Mardarich! That's right, Your Excellency. . . .
Gradoboev: If you are to be judged by the laws, we have so many laws. . . .
Sidorenko, show them how many laws we have. (Sidorenko goes out, and soon returns with a whole armful of books.) Here's how many laws! This is only how many I have, but how many more there are of them in other places! . . . And laws are always strict; they are strict in one book, and stricter in another, and strictest in the last. . . . So look, dear friends, as you wish: am I to judge you by the laws or by my feeling, as God will put it in my heart?" (Act III, Sc. 2; III, 116–17)

The easily swayed crowd accepts Gradoboev's dispositions, to his advantage. Thus he demands from a wealthy father a high ransom for his son; he releases a white-collar clerk, but has two blue-collar prisoners work out their sentence in his orchard; and the rest he returns to jail without a hearing to await judgment later. The third quasi-*samodur*, Khlynov, is far richer in this new age of capitalism than any of Ostrovsky's earlier businessmen. He is so wealthy that he waters his garden paths with champagne, and buys a cannon to fire a salute for every toast proposed by his hangers-on. His tyranny is founded not on authority, but on wealth alone. He exercises it for the new purpose of revelling with his boon companions. Like Kuroslepov, he is never sober for a moment in the course of the play.

The three monstrous *samodurs* dwarf Parasha. Yet the initial wrong solution for Kuroslepov's loss of his money in this "provincial detective story,"[10] as Lakshin calls the motor of the action, impels her to defy them and leave home. Her allies in protest are Gavrilo, her unselfish admirer, and Aristarch, who, though an idea man like Kuligin in *The Storm,* is not independent like him, since he is in Khlynov's employ. Though Parasha means to accompany Vasya when he is drafted, she finds as little support in him as Katherine did in Boris. Vasya has put his own self-interest first in allowing himself to be bought off by Khlynov: "One's own shirt is closest to one's skin," he tells Aristarch (Act IV, Tableau 1; Sc. 3; III, 139).

Along with Aristarch and Gavrilo, the gatekeeper Silan must be counted among the play's positive heroes when he sees through the wicked stepmother's disguise. Of course, the character of a wicked stepmother gives the Parasha action a fairy-tale element which critics sensed at once, calling the happy ending unrealistic. The word "warm" in the Russian title is associated with "burning," as a light burns, and so Parasha with her "warm heart" defeats the dark kingdom of *samodurstvo;* moreover, the time of the action is the dark of evening for each act except the third. Parasha stands not only for light, but also with her "heart" and with Gavrilo, who plays the guitar, for the lyric elements of love and music. Finally, in another meaning of "heart" Parasha also has courage, which she opposes to the dark oppression of her stepmother. "Take everything away from me, everything," she tells Matrena. "Only I will not give up my freedom" (Act I, Sc. 7; III, 95).

The Parasha plot has been criticized as weak. It may be, but then the possibilities of Parasha's protest have never been fully exploited. From the first performances of the play, in which the Maly Theater actor Prov Sadovsky made Kuroslepov the leading role, attention has been focused primarily on the three authoritarian monsters. Of course, Ostrovsky in their persons was attacking a *samodurstvo* which had become farcical in this later time of liberation. Even in the twentieth century and at that temple of Realism, the Moscow Art Theater, Stanislavsky staged *A Warm Heart* as a farce in his production of 1926, famous for the "humor" and "light touch" of the revelries at Khlynov's, which were said to mark Stanislavsky's achievement of Meyerholdian "theatricality." On the other hand, this play as it continued to be produced in the museum which the Moscow Art Theater had become by 1970, attained an unsurpassed low of the grotesque and repulsive in the antics of the three drunken monsters.

Surely the play deserves a new production, in this age of conscious feminism, which might emphasize not the farcical *samodurs,* but Parasha's blow for liberation, and the lyricism which Ostrovsky himself pointed up in entitling his play *A Warm Heart.*

III   *The Self-Made Man:* Easy Money *(1870)*

After the pretense at depicting an earlier age in *A Warm Heart,* Ostrovsky turns to the contemporary post-emancipation world. *Beshennye den'gi (Easy Money,* as it has become known in English, literally Mad Money, 1870), a comedy in five acts, develops the new theme of confrontation between a gentry dealing in capital, and a landed gentry impoverished for lack of it.

The hero, Vasilkov, though an aristocrat, does not belong to society. His speech reveals him as a provincial; he is also a *nouveau riche* who has made money both on the Suez Canal and in Siberia building railroads. He seeks a socialite wife who can help him attain political power. He has fallen in love with the flower of debutantes, Lidia Cheboksarova, who would normally disdain such a rough fellow except that her insane spending has so heavily drained the family estate that foreclosure threatens. For the sheer mischief of it, the scoundrel Glumov tells Lidia's mother that Vasilkov has found gold. Lidia, who to redeem the family fortunes seeks to sell herself in marriage to the highest bidder, chooses Vasilkov. Once he has paid her existing debts, she contracts still bigger ones for the wedding and establishing a stylish social life. When Vasilkov takes drastic steps to halt her extravagance, Lidia leaves him. Glumov

denounces her in an anonymous letter to her husband, who therefore suspects she has gone off with their mutual friend Telyatev. He
both challenges Telyatev to a duel and resolves to kill himself, but
Telyatev dissuades him from both intentions. Lidia returns to her
husband when the elderly Kuchumov, who had promised to keep
her in luxury, proves also to have no money. Vasilkov and Lidia
seem finally willing to work together, with the wife undertaking to
be a good housekeeper and hostess for her husband's advancement.

Of the two young men-about-town, Telyatev and Glumov, who
introduce Lidia to Vasilkov, it is Telyatev who explains the play's
title. "Easy money"—in Russian, "mad money"—is not "sensible"
or "sane" money *(umnye den'gi)*,

the money of business people, which they don't throw away for nothing. . . . Nowadays even money is sane; it all goes to business people,
and not to us. Money used to be less wise. It's just that kind of unwise
money—mad money that you need.
Lidia: What kind?
Telyatev: Mad money. That's the kind I was always getting hold of. You
can't keep hold of it. Do you know, I realized not long ago why you and I
always had mad money. Because we never earned it. Hard-earned money
is sane money. (Act V, Sc. 3; III, 238)

The aristocrat Vasilkov got his start with money from building
projects, when he even stood shoulder to shoulder on jobs with his
servant Vasily, of whom he makes a helper, not a lackey in livery.
Beside the Puritan virtues of hard work and egalitarianism, Vasilkov
represents the values of planned expenditure and simple living. He
evidently esteems honesty less for its own sake than because it pays.
"Honest calculations are the thing nowadays," he tells Glumov. "In
a practical age it is not only better to be honest, but also it pays
better" (Act I, Sc. 3; III, 173). Though he seems naive in society, he
is actually a sophisticated person who has traveled and knows
several foreign languages; moreover, he is capable of falling deeply
in love with Lidia.

Of course, his capitalist values do have a darker side. Thus he puts
his money above his love for Lidia: "I don't want to lose everything
because I love you," he tells her (Act III, Sc. 12; III, 214). After
getting on his financial feet, he has made large sums through
speculation. Like the heroes of Henry James from the same era—
rich Americans who try to storm the fort of British society—he

derives his wealth from unmentionable sources. Quite as much as the dinner to which Telyatev persuades him, the news of a successful deal, diverts him from suicide and restores his will to live. As a practical man of iron discipline, he means in the end to keep a firm rein on Lidia. He demands that she work as his housekeeper, and renouncing 'mad money,' keep within a definite budget.

Vasilkov: You know I shall not exceed our budget.
Lidia: Oh, that old budget again!
Vasilkov: Only mad money ignores a budget. (Act V, Sc. 8; III, 248)

Worst of all, Vasilkov is calculatedly ambitious, for he plans to use his wife to further his career. Thus he tells Lidia he needs her as a wife "so that I can have receptions to which I shan't be ashamed to invite ministers of state" (Act V, Sc. 7; III, 245). Vasilkov represents both the most estimable and the most reprehensible sides of capitalism.

Lidia's values are those of the society belle, though Vasilkov brings her to surrender most of them in the end. As she puts it when she finally gives in to her husband: "My goddess of carefree happiness is overthrown from her pedestal, and is replaced by a coarse idol of labor and manufacture whose name is budget" (Act, V. Sc. 7; III, 247–48). The happiness she values most depends on money: "Like a butterfly I cannot live without golden dust; I shall die . . ." (Act III, Sc. 10; III, 210). Indeed, the theme of gold runs through the play like a leitmotif, and yet Lidia is contemptuous of money:

I never knew what expensive, what cheap means; I always considered all that pitiful lower-class pennypinching. I remember once when I was coming home from a store, it occurred to me: hadn't I paid too much for a dress! I began to feel so ashamed of my thought that I blushed all over, and didn't know where to hide my face; and yet I was alone in the carriage. (Act II, Sc. 5; III, 191)

To obtain her happiness, Lidia does not hesitate to marry Vasilkov for his money, though she does not love him, as in all honesty she tells him. When he limits her spending, she resolves on resale; she will see, she says, "how strong my caress is, and that it is worth its weight in gold" (Act III, Sc. 10; III, 210). Just as wealth is to her the greatest good, so conversely "the greatest vice is poverty," as she tells her mother (ibid.).

Her mother, Nadezhda Antonovna, her confidante and coach, as well as her aristocratic environment and education have formed Lidia's character. Vasilkov accuses the aristocrat Telyatev of "corrupting" her: "In your sink of iniquity a woman can lose everything—honor, conscience, and every sense of shame" (Act IV, Sc. 9; III, 227–28). The mother launches Lidia in society with unconscionable spending, so that she may get a rich husband. To pay for his daughter's social whirl, Lidia's father has misappropriated government funds, for which he has been exiled to his estate. His wife, however, holds him up to Vasilkov as an exemplary family man for his very dishonesty: ". . . He sacrificed himself," she says, "for his sacred feelings of family love" (Act III, Sc. 12; III, 215).

Furthermore, Nadezhda Antonovna urges Lidia to sell herself to the highest bidder to save the estate from foreclosure. When Vasilkov proves to be less than a millionaire, her mother sees nothing wrong in Lidia's leaving him for a "sugar daddy" [*papashka*], which both think the elderly rake Kuchumov to be. The only advice the mother gives her daughter is "to preserve appearances" (Act IV, Sc. 4; III, 221). It is not surprising that a young woman so brought up should have exquisite and expensive tastes, but no principles.

Vasilkov's counterpart, the young man of fashion Telyatev, exerts what Gogol called "negative fascination."[11] Though the term originally referred to the devilish fascination of a Don Juan or Mephistopheles, Telyatev has the less baleful charm of an indestructible ne'er-do-well, the last scion of a dying order. He too woos Lidia, but with dishonorable intentions, as he is opposed to marriage on principle. Though he is usually without a penny in his pocket, when once by exception he has some money he offers his entire wallet with 5,000 rubles to Vasilkov. He then deprecates his generosity as "due to our general easy-going nature: when there's money around, give it to the first person you meet; when there's none—borrow from the first person you meet" (Act IV, Sc. 9; III, 227). Indeed, by the next act he needs to borrow from Vasilkov, but thinks better of it: "Better not give me any. You won't get it back, Heaven knows . . ." (Act V, Sc. 8; III, 248). In the end Telyatev does not feel his honor as a gentleman besmirched when he finds himself on his way to debtor's prison once more. Nor does he have any doubts about surviving upon his release. Like the raisonneur of classical comedy, he not only explains the meaning of the "easy money"

.

society, but also delivers the play's last verdict on its prime representatives:

Moscow is the kind of city in which we Telyatevs and Kuchumovs won't perish. Even without a cent we will have both honor and credit. For a long time to come every business man will consider himself lucky to have us sup and drink champagne at his expense. True, we won't get much respect from the tailors. But one can wear even an old overcoat and an old hat with such an air that from afar they make way for you. Farewell, dear Savva [Vasilkov]. Don't be sorry for us. (ibid.)

By and large, the play's action amounts to a straightforward nineteenth-century Russian reflection of Shakespeare's *Taming of the Shrew*. In detail, though, the plot line moves in zig-zags. In the classic reversal of the fourth act the cold and calculating careerist Vasilkov threatens a duel and suicide for love, while in the fifth Telyatev claims Vasilkov is in despair because he has presented a carriage to another woman. Is this merely a fiction Telyatev has invented to arouse Lidia's jealousy so that she will return to the husband she has left? Certainly Vasilkov makes an about-face when he resorts to cold dictates to rehabilitate his finally penitent wife.

After the play's opening critics reproached Ostrovsky for such quid-pro-quos of plot, as in a "vaudeville"; one such was his fellow writer Peter Boborykin.[12] Several found Vasilkov's character ambiguous. Was he a positive hero to be admired for the honesty and energy with which he wins out over a parasitic, decadent aristocracy? The reviewer for *Zarya* (Dawn) was unhappy that Vasilkov's business activities were not described, and the source of his wealth remained unclear.[13] Other critics likened Lidia's morals to a prostitute's. From the longer perspective of 1875, Alexander Skabichevsky praised the play, calling Vasilkov "the new type of capitalist-entrepreneur, who undoubtedly will later become the dominant figure of the dark kingdom."[14] But the critic of *Novoe vremya* (New Time) at the play's opening accused Ostrovsky of reinforcing through Vasilkov the attitudes of the very *samodurs* whom "he castigates."[15]

Certainly Ostrovsky here depicts a social stratum different from those he has described before, with problems peculiar to a new age, epitomized in the apt metaphor of the title. Again an open ending poses the question: Will Lidia learn? Still, the question is not so open as before, for the victory is clearly Vasilkov's. There is little to choose in the end, though, between a moribund aristocracy which can only spend money it has not earned and a nascent capitalism which deifies budgets and hard work, while borrowing and speculating in huge sums. Or must the viewer in the end inevitably applaud success over failure?

IV *"The Ideal and Life"*: The Forest *(1871)*

Like *Easy Money, Les* (The Forest, 1871) exposes widespread cupidity, especially that of the decadent aristocrat and *samodur* Gurmyzhskaya, who is selling her forests to the former peasant and lumber profiteer Vosmibratov. Though she pretends the cash so realized will go to charity, she actually intends to cheat her nephew and heir out of his inheritance in land, and use the money for herself. She declares that her ward Aksyusha must marry Bulanov, a callow youth, the son of her widowed friend, who will benefit by the girl's dowry. Vosmibratov cheats Gurmyzhskaya out of a thousand rubles of the sum agreed upon for two forest tracts. He also proposes that she give Aksyusha a dowry of 3,000 rubles and marry her to his son Peter, a suggestion which Gurmyzhskaya indignantly rejects, though the young couple is in love.

The nephew, sent early into the world without a penny for his education, has worked for fifteen years as an actor of tragic roles under the name Neschastlivtsev (Unhappy). Now, accompanied by a comic actor Arkashka called Schastlivtsev (Happy), he comes home to see his aunt, though he pretends to the more honorable calling of a retired army officer, and makes Arkashka play the part of his valet. With the grand manner of an actor, he recovers for his aunt the thousand rubles due her from Vosmibratov. When Arkashka tells Neschastlivtsev that he has overheard the aunt making a gift of the money to the schoolboy Bulanov, the nephew has too much respect for his aunt to believe it. In revenge for Neschastlivtsev's making a liar and a lackey of him, Arkashka gives away their true identity, which leads to their nearly being driven from the estate.

Meanwhile, Aksyusha asks the supposed officer for 2,000 rubles, the sum Vosmibratov will now accept as her dowry to marry Peter, but Neschastlivtsev finds himself unfortunately penniless. Incredulous that his aunt could treat him thus, he forces from her a single payment of a thousand rubles in return for renouncing his inheritance forever, which money Arkashka and he plan to squander on high living. However, hearing Gurmyzhskaya then announce her engagement to Bulanov, and also refuse to give her ward a penny, her nephew uses his thousand to pay the again reduced price of Aksyusha's dowry. After so buying her happiness of Vosmibratov, the actors depart on foot, as they had come.

The figure of Gurmyzhskaya recalls characters from Ostrovsky's earlier plays. Her estate is five kilometers from Kalinov, scene of *The Storm* and *A Warm Heart*. Before her little court of friends and servants she gives herself the airs of a hypocritical *samodur*, like Turusina in *The Diary of a Scoundrel*. Yet her *samodurstvo* has assumed tendencies peculiar to the new capitalist age. She and her male partner *samodur* Vosmibratov are devastating the forest for cash, and her estate is appropriately named The Stumps. A forest crossroads, at which the two actors meet, with its road sign pointing one way to Kalinov, the other to The Stumps, is described thus: "At the mile marker a broad low stump, and behind it a triangular clearing between the roads covered with stubbly thicket no taller than a man" (stage direction for Act II; III, 268).

While such earlier *samodurs* as Kabanikha and Dikoy ruthlessly exercised authority for its own sake, Gurmyzhskaya uses hers for self-indulgence, which she conceals behind the mask of sweet charity. Like the postemancipation Turusina, she too seeks the approval of her little retinue; at the play's beginning she invites them to the signing of her will two days hence, as if she were not long for this world. Indeed, with her eyes thus hypocritically cast up to heaven, she has been called Madame Tartuffe. Two days later, when her friends return in the last act, they witness her engagement instead. She is marrying the stupid boy Bulanov, who, like the hero of Denis Fonvizin's classic comedy *The Minor*, has not managed even to finish school.

The brief time lapse in the play of only forty-eight hours, as well as its five acts, are the outward signs of its classic form. Certain "speaking names" are also in the classic tradition: for example, among Gurmyzhskaya's friends the flatterer Milonov (Mr. Nice), and the opinionated Bodaev (Mr. Blunt or Bullhead). As might be expected from their names, the two express opposite opinions; thus Milonov terms Gurmyzhskaya's stinginess in depriving her nephew of an education an admirable strict simplicity, while Bodaev, on the contrary, remarks that "you don't get anything without paying for it" (Act I, Sc. 4; III, 257). Further, Bodaev refuses to rationalize her admission of having wronged her nephew by selling some of the land belonging to his inheritance; instead her blunt courtier observes that ". . . women have brought final ruin to many noble estates" (Act I, Sc. 5; III, 260). Classic conventions thus frame a satiric picture of topical reference. The *samodur* Gurmyzhskaya is not only diminished by her own weakness, but also challenged as Kabanikha never was. The lumber dealer Vosmibratov dares to propose crossing class lines when he asks for her relative Aksyusha's hand for his son, and a dowry of 4,000 rubles, his first asking price, to boot. When Gurmyzhskaya decrees Aksyusha's engagement to Bulanov instead, her dictate does not go unchallenged. Aksiusha flatly refuses.

Aksiusha: I shan't marry him. . . .
Gurmyzhskaia: How do you dare? . . . You don't have the right to enter into my intentions: I need to have it so, and that's all. He's your intended, and you his fiancée,—only you will stay in your room under supervision. I have so decided!
Aksiusha (staring her in the eye): Is that all?
Gurmyzhskaia: That's all, you may go. (Act I, Sc. 7; III, 265–66)

Like Aksyusha, who stares down her aunt, Peter, too, has not been crushed by their subordination to *samodurs*, but has plans for resisting.

Beside such challengers as Gurmyzhskaya's stubborn neighbor, her lumber merchant and her ward, even her toadying servant Ulita deplores the caste system which she holds responsible for her own sycophancy. But Gurmyzhskaia's major challenger is her nephew, and his progression from admiration to contempt traces a major plot line of the play.

The two actors who come to the estate in the second tableau of Act II provide the outsider's viewpoint from which the *samodurstvo* of the forest is exposed. They bring to bear on it not only the outside point of view, but also the ideals of literature, their daily stock in trade. True, the comedian admits the few books he carries in his backpack are farces, but the tragedian has the costume of Hamlet in his pack and Hamlet's words on his lips, and he uses Schiller's ranting eloquence in berating his aunt in the end.

Still their challenge of Gurmyzhskaia does not represent the pure Schillerian antithesis of "The Ideal and Life."[16] For at the same time the two are only poor devils of wandering actors, the outcasts of bourgeois society, with the marks of their kind—an overly great liking for the bottle, and not a penny to their names. The younger man, Neschastlivtsev, still longs for the respite of a stay at home, but the older, Schastlivtsev, knows that "you can't go home again," because he once tried it: despite the comfortable living, he suffered so from the gloom and boredom of the middle-class milieu that he ran away a second time, on this occasion with a full awareness of his calling. He has also gone further than Neschastlivtsev on the downward path of an aging actor's career. After playing the young lover at first, he went on to act as fall-guy in farce, then to imitate bird-calls; finally, he fears, he will be demoted from the stage to the prompter's box. Both men are wholly improvident.

Yet Neschastlivtsev dreams of organizing his own acting company, for which he tries to recruit Aksyusha, as if the capacity for feeling she shows by attempting suicide were enough to qualify her as an actress. Furthermore, for all his awareness of his gypsy status, he has known the power of the ideal in art. As he describes it to Aksyusha: "I'm a poor, penniless tramp, but on stage I'm a prince. I live his life, suffer from his thoughts, weep his tears over unhappy Ophelia, and love her as forty thousand brothers are incapable of loving" (Act IV, Sc. 6; III, 313).

In the name of the ideal nobility of art he challenges the real nobles of Gurmyzhskaya's retinue: "Comedians?" he asks of those who would ignobly show his friend and him the door.

No, we are artists, noble artists—it is you who are comedians. If we love, then we show it; . . . if we give help, then down to our last hard-earned penny. And you? You discuss all your lives the welfare of society, the love of mankind. And what have you done? . . . Whom have you comforted? You comfort only yourselves. You are the comedians, the clowns, not we. (Act V, Sc. 9; III, 337)

From Schiller's first play *in tyrannos*, *The Robbers*, he takes his condemnation of their *samodurstvo*: "People, people! Brood of crocodiles! Your tears are water! Your hearts, hard armor! . . . Oh, could I but turn to stone before this hellish tribe of blood-thirsty inhabitants of the forest!" (ibid.). From this, then, derives the metaphor of the play's title: the barbarous jungle or forest with its inhabitants of unfeeling respectability.

The ring of Schiller's idealistic rhetoric is intermingled with the comic dignity of the Don Quixote–Sancho Panza pair who quote *The Robbers* in parting. With their departure ends not only their plot

line, but also those of the other two pairs, Peter-Aksyusha and
Gurmyzhskaya-Bulanov. In this perhaps most artful of Ostrovsky's
endings, not only does the actors' plot line come full circle when
they leave on foot as they came, but the lines of the other two
couples are entwined as the money passes from hand to hand until
it, too, ends up where it started. That is, Vosmibratov withheld the
sum of a thousand rubles from the amount due Gurmyzhskaya, but
disgorged it under pressure from Neschastlivtsev, who returned it
to his aunt, who first gave it to Bulanov, but then was blackmailed
by the actor into giving it to him, who made a present of it to
Aksyusha for her dowry, which came again into Vosmibratov's
hands.

Of course, the double wedding of Bulanov to Gurmyzhskaya and
Peter to Aksyusha follows the stereotype of the classic comedy
ending, which the American critic Mary McCarthy calls "a happy
wrapping up usually signified by a marriage or multiple marriages. . . . This glad wrapping up of an awful tangle of cross-
purposes is improbable and often incredible. . . . The pairing off
that signals the finale of *Love's Labour Lost* (or *The Marriage of
Figaro*) makes us laugh and clap because, among other things, it is
so funny, too Noah's ark good to be true."[17] If taken seriously, the
two marriages at the end of *The Forest* are not "too good," but "too
bad to be true." Both bride and groom have been "had" in the
absurd pairing of the old woman and the schoolboy. Even Peter and
Aksyusha would be better off leaving the forest, which Neschastlivtsev has unmistakably placed on the map of "the dark
kingdom."

In his great reinterpretation of *The Forest* (1924), Meyerhold had
the young couple do just that—set off for a new life of freedom—just
as he made of his whole production a revolutionary manifesto of
early Bolshevik enthusiasm.

Even in Ostrovsky's lifetime *The Forest* was markedly successful,
although its initial production at the Alexandrinsky was poor. Feeling it to be a strong play, Ostrovsky presented it for an Uvarov
Prize, but it was rejected, surely because it excoriates in the
aristocracy a caste as outlived as feudalism. In his 1926 essays on the
old Russia, Vladimir Gilyarovsky identifies the prototypes of the two
actors, one of whom—Nikolay Rybakov (Neschastlivtsev)—superbly
played the role, in which the character mentions an actor Rybakov
(III, 276). *The Forest* has been Ostrovsky's most often produced

play, not only because of the excellent roles it provides but also because of its profound reflection of the provincial actor's life.

Finally, *The Forest* again exposes the decay of "the dark kingdom" in a decadent aristocracy through a ringing challenge derived from the great ideals of literature. The actor who, alone in Ostrovsky's plays, delivers that challenge becomes a champion of humanity against an outmoded social order.

V *Warm or Cold Heart?* Late Love *(1874)*

Discussion of *Pozdniaia liubov'* (Late Love), written the same year as *The Snow Maiden* (1873), has more than once been launched with a passage from Ostrovsky's letter to Turgenev of June 14, 1874, in which he looks back on both recently completed plays after reviewing the French translation of *The Storm* before its production in Paris: "Now I can 'make' a play only a little worse than the French."[18] He is referring to the French "well-made play," with the carefully contrived plot characteristic of such authors as Émile Augier or Victorien Sardou. Certainly *Late Love* has been criticized for the artificiality of its plot. Indeed, Ostrovsky's plays of the 1870s generally have been criticized for their complicated action, the exact opposite of the aimless structure, or even lack of such, which had made both the fame and blame of his early "scenes" of Moscow life.

Late Love is also subtitled "scenes"—"Scenes of Unsophisticated Life" in four acts—because all its characters are nonaristocrats, except Lebedkina, a lady with whom the young lawyer Nikolay Shablov is infatuated. So as to court her in her society world, he has gone into debt. When he sends to his mother for thirty rubles which he has lost gambling, the mother does not have that much. Instead, their neighbor Lyudmila dispatches a fifty-ruble note, all that she has, though this is money which her father has entrusted to her for safekeeping.

Lyudmila keeps the money and papers of her father Margaritov, a bill collector, because years before, when robbed of a promissory note by a clerk, he had spent a lifetime making restitution for the amount of the lost note. Now he is to collect Lebedkina's debt for Dorodnov, who considers its collection so unlikely that he will accept half the 6,000 rubles due, leaving the other half as a bonus for the collector. The dishonest Lebedkina, who forged her husband's signature as guarantor to start with, does not mean to pay now if she

can help it. She tells Nikolay to get the document back from
Lyudmila, since she knows the girl will do anything for love of him.
Upon its return Lebedkina promises to pay Nikolay half the amount
of her debt.

Lyudmila gives Nikolay Lebedkina's IOU, hoping to save him
from debtor's prison with the amount the lady has promised for the
return of her note, and to keep him from using the revolver she
discovers he has bought in despair. But when Nikolay returns the
note, Lebedkina laughs at her promise and burns the IOU, thus
.estroying all claim upon her, and making Nikolay, Lyudmila, and
Margaritov in honor liable for the debt. However, Nikolay reveals
that the note Lebedkina burned was only a copy, and she must now
pay. Margaritov gives his share of the sum collected to Lyudmila as
her dowry, which she brings to Nikolay, who marries her, pays his
debt, and takes over Margaritov's firm.

Like *The Forest, Late Love* uses money as the mainspring of its
action. Obtaining the money needed to save the young lovers
depends upon the selfish caprice of an older upper-class woman,
who can afford to pay her debt but would prefer not to. The
aristocrat Lebedkina is rather a siren than a *samodur* like Gurmyzhskaya, for she has charmed Nikolay into falling in love with
her. True, he might be more in love with the high life he can lead
with her, escaping thus from the sordid lower-class milieu he shares
with the other characters. His need of money for society life with
her impels every step of the action until she breaks her promise to
him, thus curing him of his love. Again, as in *The Forest*, a sum of
money circulates through many hands until with its payment as
dowry the happiness of a young couple is achieved in the end.

Despite the play's casual designation as "scenes," each of the four
acts moves to an effective conclusion. The first three bring Nikolay
ever closer to ruin, and evoke ever more decisive reactions from
Lyudmila to each step of his descent. The first ends with Lyudmila's
generosity in sending fifty rubles from her father's funds in response
to Nikolay's desperate request for thirty to pay his gambling loss. At
the end of the second she faints on learning that he is threatened
with debtor's prison. At the third act curtain she unhesitatingly
gives him Lebedkina's note from her father's portfolio for safekeeping. Her betrayal of her father in Act III—which in a classic five-act
drama would represent the central turning point of the action—
should initiate a turn for the better in Nikolay's downward course.
The surprise usual in Act IV of the classic play, as well as the

denouement, occur in the last of these four acts. The surprise is the disclosure that Lebedkina has burned only a copy of her note, though the happy ending is almost equally surprising, namely Mary McCarthy's "Noah's ark pairing off " of Nikolay and Lyudmila. The dullard clerk at Margaritov's and Nikolay's younger brother Dormedont, whose honest love Lyudmila has passed over throughout the play, remains as an odd third, but he resigns himself to doing chores and minding the children in his brother's house.

Ostrovsky's friend Burdin criticized what he considered the transparency of the trick Nikolay plays on Lebedkina, foreseeing that audiences must guess she burns only a copy. Ostrovsky denied that the trick was obvious, and argued that Burdin had misunderstood the play if he thought Lebedkina and her IOU were its central focus. Instead, he wrote that "the essential action of the play is in Nikolay and Lyudmila."[19]

The characters of Nikolay and Lyudmila hardly support closer consideration, though. They are one-directional, capable at best of an about-face. Through three acts Nikolay is drawn to Lebedkina as to a lodestone; and what is incredible is less the ruse he employs with her than the fact that he musters sufficient scepticism about her to use it. His change of heart toward Lyudmila, if not incredible, at least is hidden from the audience, doubtless so as to keep the existence of the copy a secret. For if Lyudmila's prompt return of the IOU converts him to her side, he says only, as the curtain falls on Act III, "Now I know what I must do" (Act III, Sc. 7; IV, 46).

Certainly Lyudmila moves in only one direction as if under hypnosis throughout the play. She appropriates her father's money to pay Nikolay's gambling debt, and for Nikolay's sake she hands over the note entrusted to her father for collection. Both these thefts from her father she justifies through her love, as also she does her turning to Nikolay away from Margaritov: "Fate has bound me to him [Nikolay] . . . what am I to do," she explains helplessly to her father. "I see, I feel that I am killing you. . . . I too am dying, but I am his . . ." (Act IV, Sc. 6; IV, 55).

Just as the complicated plot and surprise ending are typical of the later Ostrovsky of the 1870s, in contrast to the plotless play and open ending typical of the younger dramatist, so all-sacrificing love like Lyudmila's is frequent among the heroines of this later decade. The warm-hearted Parasha of the previous decade, like Lyudmila, sets things right by doing wrong—in her case running away—but her wrong-doing had a cause in her father's oppression, and could have no harmful consequence for anyone but herself. Lyudmila, however, wrongs a kind father, which could have ruinous consequences for them both. When all nevertheless turns out for the best, the ending seems contrived.

Ostrovsky apparently considered the lower-class milieu a sufficient explanation for Nikolay's enchantment with Lebedkina and her very different world. The author not only equipped the play with what is perhaps the longest place description in all his work, he also insisted that a new set be especially designed and constructed for the Maly Theater production of *Late Love*. Further, he had the curtain rise on the empty set so that the audience could take in the lower-class, unsophisticated setting—or *zakholust'e*, as it is called in the subtitle—before any actors entered. Lyudmila has made her peace with life in this "poor, time-darkened room" at the Shablovs', as the initial stage direction describes it (IV, 8). In the second act, the classic "wind-up" of the action, she tells Nikolay: "I had gotten the upper hand of myself, and was . . . happy in my way. . . . This, though, is my late, perhaps my last love; . . . I shall be content if I can make your life easier in any way, comfort you" (Act II, Sc. 3; IV, 28). Nikolay then explains why he has come to feel so "broken" as to buy the revolver which Lyudmila notices in his pocket: he is not "hopelessly in love," nor has he "misappropriated public funds"; rather, he tells her quite simply, "there's no reason to live" (Act II, Sc. 3; IV, 29). Of course, no sooner does Lebedkina invite him for a ride in her carriage than he again rushes off with her away from his sad milieu, despite his promise to Lyudmila to rest at home and recover. Can the need to escape from the poor dark room in his mother's house explain his ruinous course into the brighter world?

Ostrovsky again underlines the importance of the milieu in the motivation of his characters with his remark, in a memo of 1884, that a set exists, not just for the splendor of a dramatic production, or for the sake of verisimilitude, but, above all, for the comprehension of character: "Just as in life we understand people better if we see the circumstances in which they live, so too on the stage a true-to-life environment acquaints us at once with the situation of the characters, and makes the types portrayed . . . more comprehensible for the audience."[20]

In the same memo Ostrovsky reports that the actor Sergey Shumsky, who played Margaritov in the Maly production of *Late Love*, praised the special new set: "I remember how Shumsky thanked the designer [Pavel] Isakov for the small, poor room in the play *Late Love*. 'You don't even have to act in it,' he said. 'In it you can live. I no sooner entered on stage than I fell into the right tone.' "[21]

However persuasive the single setting may be, though, it hardly suffices to motivate Nikolay's and Lyudmila's actions entirely. Moreover, like every single setting of a classic play which observes the three unities, it raises the difficulty of bringing everyone to Shablova's "poor room." Lebedkina comes supposedly to have her fortune told by Nikolay's mother, Shablova. But it is harder to accept the supposition that Margaritov's business—the agreement with Dorodnov concerning Lebedkina's IOU—is also transacted there, unless to satisfy a convention of the classic play.

The modern Soviet critics Kholodov and Lakshin both insist that such technique of the "well-made" play is subordinated to the impressive Realism of *Late Love*. Kholodov, for example, shows that Margaritov's melodramatic theories to explain his daughter's misconduct are unnecessary: "What devils have they conjured up from hell to deceive and flatter your righteous soul?" (Act IV, Sc. 6; IV, 54). Rather the power of money in the capitalist society of the time compels her to undertake desperate measures to save Nikolay. As Margaritov describes it, "they steal and sell everything. If you need to buy a man to forge or commit a crime, or buy a girl's honor—come here, and it's for sale and cheap" (Act II, Sc. 1; IV, 23). Lakshin, too, attributes the intensification of plot interest and melodrama to the reality of the time. Ostrovsky learned of financial scandals and increasing moral corruption not only from newspapers, but also from his duties as honorary judge of civil court in Kineshma, and later, as a grand juror of Moscow Circuit Court. His continued faithful depiction of reality became willy-nilly as devious and melodramatic as contemporary reality itself.

One critic among the playwright's contemporaries, Goncharov, in the posthumously published, "Materials for a Critical Article on Ostrovsky," remarked that the dramatist's recent plays had not merited the cold critical reception they received. Indeed, "his latest—*Late Love*," Goncharov wrote, "could be reckoned among his best works."[22] Vladimir Nemirovich-Danchenko, Stanislavsky's partner in creating the Chekhovian Realism of the Moscow Art Theater, valued *Late Love* very highly, not only in the Ostrovsky canon—in technical mastery above *The Storm, A Poor Bride* and *Easy Money*—but also in Russian literature overall: "In general after *The Inspector General* these two plays [*Fiancée without Fortune* and *Late Love*] are almost the most remarkable in their technique."[23] Very possibly the idea of "living on stage" afforded by the all-important milieu, a notion so close to the Stanislavskian Method, might in itself explain Nemirovich-Danchenko's high opinion of *Late Love*. To this quality should be added the play's thesis—the triumph of honesty—and yet a third great quality much praised in a contemporary newspaper review, its admirable rendering of typical speech.

Despite what contemporary and modern critics have said, *Late Love* suffers from a contrived plot and superficial, unilinear characters. It is another runaround in rubles, but without the depth and complexity of *The Forest's* threefold plot, or its high ideal of humanity. No wonder *Late Love* is not among Ostrovsky's more frequently produced plays.

VI   *Even the Dog Is Eaten Alive:* Wolves and Sheep *(1875)*

Undoubtedly a major play, *Volki i ovtsy* (Wolves and Sheep, 1875), is one of three works by Ostrovsky showing life on country estates under the unjust rule, or *samodurstvo*, of women owners. The owner in this play, Murzavetskaya, unlike the owners in the two earlier plays, *The Ward* and *The Forest*, commits crimes of extortion and forgery modeled on an actual case: the extortion—ostensibly for charity—by Abbess Mitrofany of 2 million rubles from a business man's wife, for which the abbess was sentenced in 1874 to Siberia. Before entering the convent the abbess had been Baroness Rozen, daughter of a general highly placed at court. Presumably Ostrovsky transferred the action of his play from court and convent to the world, not so much to avoid censorship, as to depict ordinary life rather than an extraordinary case.

With her estate deeply in debt, Murzavetskaya keeps the creditors from her door by inducing her recently widowed neighbor, Kupavina, to pay her sums supposedly owed by the late Kupavin. Chugunov, both Kupavina's and Murzavetskaya's manager, who procured the husband's forged signature on which the young woman paid a thousand, persuades her further to sign a blank promissory note to cover additional sums allegedly owed the Murzavetskys. However, Murzavetskaya offers to forego payment of the second note if Kupavina will marry Apollon Murzavetsky, the old woman's drunken misfit of a nephew.

Kupavina's old friend Lynyaev suspects both promises to pay

have been forged. In his quest to prove this he finds an unexpected ally in Glafira, Murzavetskaya's companion, whom the old woman has placed as a spy at Kupavina's. Glafira, who has set her cap at Lynyaev, strikes a bargain with him. She leads him to the forger, Chugunov's nephew, in return for which he must pretend to woo her. Once he has gone this far, she ensnares him as her husband.

Meanwhile Kupavina, whose entire estate could be forfeit for the blank check she signed, has sought the help of a St. Petersburg financier, Berkutov. Though more in love with her estate than her, Berkutov gets back her note by threatening to expose Murzavetskaya, marries the young woman, and gains the support of the old one to become a power in the province.

Though Murzavetskaya's influence is unusual, her hopeless indebtedness was an all too usual situation of the estate owner in the postemancipation age, and motivates her assault upon the rich widow's property, which she will acquire if she can blackmail her into marriage with Apollon. Lynyaev epitomizes these inhuman relations by an apt metaphor in a conversation with Murzavetskaya:

Lynyaev: Do you think people live around us?
Murzavetskaya: Why, who do you think does?
Lynyaev: Wolves and sheep. The wolves devour the sheep, and the sheep peacefully let themselves be devoured. (Act I, Sc. 10; IV, 134)

Murzavetskaya accepts her categorization as a wolf; she'd prefer it, she says, to being a sheep in the same herd with Lynyaev.

Murzavetskaya's manager Chugunov sides with her, and not with his other employer Kupavina. Only he disputes the word "wolf," saying: "What sort of wolves are we? We're doves, chickens . . . pecking a grain of corn at a time. . . . They're the wolves! They gobble up big bites" (Act V, Sc. 12; IV, 206). The real wolves, in his view, are Berkutov, who carried off Kupavina, and Glafira, who swallowed up Lynyaev.

Certainly Glafira may be reckoned among the wolves in the end, though overall she must be rated the most enigmatic person in the play. True, Ostrovsky's attitude toward her is clearer than it was toward Lidia Cheboksarova in *Easy Money*, whose situation resembles hers. Well-born, with a name meaning in Greek "elegant," Glafira lacked money to continue after her debut with a round of balls and parties in St. Petersburg, and had to become Murzavetskaya's companion in the provinces. At first she plays the part of a shy schoolgirl, wearing black, as if about to enter a convent. She frankly confesses her intentions toward Lynyaev to Kupavina, who helps by lending her elegant dresses and furthering her meetings with Lynyaev.

That Berkutov is a wolf is plain almost immediately, yet his name, which has caught Kupavina's fancy from afar, confirms a certain dash. *Berkut* means in Russian a golden eagle, a great bird capable of killing a wolf. Berkutov, a predator himself, drives off the wolf Murzavetskaya so as to seize her prey. He has instilled doubt in Kupavina before his arrival by writing her not to initiate any changes on the estate without his advice. He is quite frank with Lynyaev:

Berkutov: I came only to get married.
Lynyaev: To whom?
Berkutov: To Madame Kupavina.
Lynyaev: You mean it's all settled?
Berkutov: It hasn't begun yet.
Lynyaev: It hasn't begun yet, and you already speak with such assurance?
Berkutov: I see no reason to doubt. Oh, I have had my eye out for a long time.
Lynyaev: On Madame Kupavina?
Berkutov: No, on her estate—well, of course on her too.

(Act IV, Sc. 3; IV, 177)

Amazingly, Berkutov then coldly advises Kupavina to marry Murzavetsky, painting a dark picture of the consequences if she does not. Does he mean to make her plight seem the more desperate, so as to set off his rescue of her the more starkly? For he does rescue Kupavina by threatening Murzavetskaya with exposure. But then again he stops short at the threat, and lets her advise him to stand for public office in the province, and to marry Kupavina. When the latter, with Murzavetskaya's encouragement, confesses her love, he proposes marriage in a manner better suited to a Rockefeller than a Romeo: "I beg you to make me your manager . . ." (Act V, Sc. 9; IV, 203). Indeed, before seeing the lady he has told Lynyaev of his plans for her estate: to start a distillery, and to profit by his advance information that a railroad soon to be built will greatly increase the value of the land.

Both Kupavina and Lynyaev aspire to keep their freedom, she to manage her own estate, he as a confirmed bachelor rather resembling Goncharov's indolent Oblomov. But both are lambs to the slaughter of the wolves who prey upon them.

For all its stern depiction of the aristocracy, the play is genuinely a comedy. One strand of the twofold action—the designing Glafira's capture of the reluctant bachelor Lynyaev in marriage—is as comic as such an intrigue has always been throughout a long tradition, including Beatrice's entrapment of Benedick in Shakespeare's *Much Ado About Nothing*, or the near-ensnarement of Gogol's Podkolesin in *The Marriage*. The newlyweds' departure for Paris at the end of *Wolves and Sheep* was played in superbly comic fashion by the nineteenth-century actor Alexander Lensky as Lynyaev: as Glafira tells how he esteems her self-effacing humility above all else, she marshals him to her service, tossing him cape, scarf, and umbrella, until he stands laden with her things like a Christmas tree. Just then coffee is offered him, but he must plaintively refuse a cup, not having a free hand to take one.

Two of the best comic roles are those of lesser characters. Kupavina's Aunt Anfusa, the poor relative who earns her keep by pouring tea, chaperoning, and generally doing as she is told, exhibits the result of lifelong subordination by her inability to utter more than monosyllables. One of her typical speeches reads: "Yes, right . . . from his journey . . . and I surely . . ." (Act V, Sc. 7; IV, 200).

Aunt Anfusa possesses not only her own peculiar character beyond that of the classic maid or confidante; she also has a function in the plot: Kupavina, in fleeing the play's other most comic character, the drunken suitor Murzavetsky, leaves Aunt Anfusa behind in a rearguard action to fend him off. But Murzavetsky is so far gone in drink that he sees two Anfusas:

Murzavetsky: Pardon ladies! (Looking around) Oh, there they are! Apparently both of them. It's as if something is clouding my eyes, something is moving: now one lady, now two . . . no, two, two . . . well, of course, two. (Bowing from afar) My respects.
Anfusa (turning away): Well, so . . . please, don't, so. . . .
(Act III, Sc. 5; IV, 163)

The comedy of Murzavetsky's role derives from the emptiness of his heroic mask. Nominally an officer and an aristocrat, he has been let go from the service, and now devotes his life to wheedling a drink, or money for a drink, from anyone and everyone. In his befuddled encounter with Anfusa he protests Romantic love to one of the two, whom he takes for Kupavina, only to discover she is not.

Even his dog, as foolish as he but bearing the heroic name of Tamerlane, manages, though close to town and in broad daylight, to be eaten alive by wolves. Like master like man; a wolf is overtaken by a sheepish fate. This play is also highly structured, without, however, seeming too contrived for a comedy. Its two plot lines are reflected in two places of action: Murzavetskaya's, where the first and last acts are set; and Kupavina's, where the central three acts take place. In itself alone this disposition of the acts should raise Murzavetskaya and Kupavina to due importance as the antagonists in the conflict between "wolves and sheep," despite Kholodov's contention that Glafira is the play's heroine. She is rather one of the two predators from outside; she devours Lynyaev, just as Berkutov does Kupavina. In view of Berkutov's major role in the other plot strand, parallel to Glafira's, it is amazing that he does not appear until the fourth act, and then as the classic surprise, or new element in that act. Act IV does indeed surprise by temporarily reversing the course of both plot lines: Murzavetskaya sends her carriage to fetch Glafira away from her pursuit of Lynyaev, and Berkutov tells Kupavina she should marry the nephew. Both reverse actions culminate in the double wedding of the last act, though the predators are not thereby frustrated, as in classic comedy, but instead fulfilled.

If in one sense both plot lines are thus finally unraveled in the denouement of the double wedding, in another sense the ending is an open one. The perpetrators of the forgery, Chugunov and his nephew Goretsky, feel as little guilt for their wrongdoing as Yusov did for his in A Profitable Post, as if ethics were a luxury of the upper classes. Goretsky is sent off to forge ahead elsewhere. Chugunov receives a thousand rubles' gratuity for renouncing the coup of Kupavina's total ruin, and will undoubtedly continue in his wicked ways. The presumptuous old matriarch Murzavetskaya is reaffirmed as arbiter of fate for the whole county; as she says: "I love to know everything in the world, and poke my nose into everything that goes on where I'm not wanted" (Act V, Sc. 8; IV, 201).

Some critics of the play, upon its publication and before its performance, saw in it only a reworking of the scandalous event on which it was based; others viewed it as a "pamphlet," as indeed it is, satirizing a corrupt aristocracy. But then, extremely well acted in both major cities, it became an immediate success in performance, and has since remained among Ostrovsky's more frequently produced plays.

In sum, *Wolves and Sheep* reflects its ruthless age of loans and land deals, railroad construction, and the founding of industrial enterprises. It creates superb comedy of character and situation realized through skillful development of plot and dialogue. Yet, except for the good nature of Kupavina and Lynyaev, it shows more human failing than feeling. Even hardheaded Lidia and crass Vasil-kov in *Easy Money* exhibit positive feeling for each other by the end, whereas their counterparts in *Wolves and Sheep* seem devoid of even negative feeling. Only the scheming old Murzavetskaya displays the latter in all her vengeful meanness, and continues to loom large at the end, thanks to her all too human faults.

CHAPTER 6

Last But Not Least

I   *To Love Not Wisely But Too Well:* The Final Sacrifice *(1878)*

IN *Posledniaia zhertva* (The Final Sacrifice, 1878), Ostrovsky has
again written a drama, not "a comedy in five acts," as he terms it.
For although the play ends in the manner of classic comedy with the
expectation of two weddings, both negate Romantic love, and affirm
instead the power of money.

A distant relative of the young widow Julia Tugina, the rich old
millionaire Pribytkov [Mr. Profit], offers to manage her money and
make her his companion, by which he means his mistress. She
indignantly refuses because she loves Dulchin, to whom she has
gradually given everything she inherited from her late husband.
Now that she has mortgaged her last property, he asks her to save
him from debtor's prison, and she must make "the final sacrifice" of
begging Pribytkov for the 6,000 rubles Dulchin needs, in return for
which her lover again promises to marry her. Aunt Glafira and
Pribytkov devise a plan to save Julia from Dulchin: Pribytkov will
suggest his intention of generously endowing his grandniece Irina,
who is in love with Dulchin; the prospect of her dowry will enable
her to snare Dulchin away from Julia.

Indeed, just as Julia is making her wedding preparations she
learns that Dulchin, instead of paying his debt, has gambled away
the 6,000 rubles. She also receives an invitation to the party
celebrating his engagement to Irina. Julia thereupon sinks into a
faint resembling death.

Thinking to elope, Irina goes to Dulchin, but when he discovers
her dowry is only 5,000, he sends her home. He intends to ask Julia
again for money, but the news of her apparent death, for which he
believes himself to blame, makes him briefly consider suicide. She,
however, enters on the arm of her fiancé, Pribytkov, who promises

to sue Dulchin for the large sum he owes Julia; this compels him to sell himself in marriage to the rich widow Pivokurova (Mrs. Brewery).

Undoubtedly Ostrovsky meant this conclusive—not open—ending as a surprise, for he made sure the play was staged in both Moscow and St. Petersburg in the fall of 1877 before it was published in Saltykov-Shchedrin's *Otechestvennye zapiski* for January of 1878. He further complained in a letter to Burdin that a St. Petersburg newspaper, after a reading of the play at Burdin's house, had published a plot summary of the play: "Let them only evaluate, but to tell the story of a play which derives half its interest from the unexpected! Where is it proper to do that?"[1]

The plot with its final surprise related to the "well-made play" may seem contrived, but it is not complicated. Indeed the plot line is as classically simple as the unilinear action of Pierre Racine's tragedy *Andromaque*, in which all the characters are lined up one behind another, each longing for the one ahead: Hermione loves Pyrrhus, who loves Andromaque, who loves the dead Hector, or the surrogate in his place, their son Astyanax. In Ostrovsky's play Pribytkov courts Julia, who loves Dulchin, whose heart is set on gambling and pleasure, or on anyone who will provide him with funds therefor. The action then consists in about-faces of the characters toward, or away from one another, until all the possible combinations of couples have been exhausted.

The exposition in the first act uses as timeworn a device as the butler's telling the maid what both already know about the master and the mistress: that is, in *The Final Sacrifice* Aunt Glafira, who has come to call, interrogates Julia's housekeeper. In Act II, in which "the plot thickens," Dulchin begins the about-face by asking Julia for money, and so causing Julia to turn to Pribytkov. In Act III Dulchin has turned away again to court Irina at the great garden party. In Act IV Julia is astonished to receive the announcement of her intended's engagement to another; when Pribytkov enters, she turns to him in near delirium, then faints. The scene then shifts, a familiar device to maintain suspense over Julia's fate. At Dulchin's the newly affianced young couple meet and reject each other; the young man, who was about to ask Julia again for money, must turn definitely toward her when he hears from Glafira that she is dead. The final turnabout comes with Julia's surprise appearance in the company of Pribytkov. Dulchin must pair off with Pivokurova if he is to redeem the sheaf of IOUs with which the newly engaged couple

Pribytkov and Julia confront him. The course of the five acts and the action conform thus to the scheme of the classic tragedy of Racine.

Yet this line graph of the action is fleshed out with the Realism by which Ostrovsky made his reputation. For example, though Act III, as in the classic scheme, represents the turning point, when Dulchin decisively turns away from Julia to become engaged to Irina, it also presents a panorama of the Moscow rich at play. Beside Dulchin and his shabby friend Dergachev, the Pribytkovs, the moneylender Salay Saltanych and the rich widow Pivokurova, those present are largely nameless personages: "a visitor from another city," "a Moscow man," "an observer," "a gossip," "three gambler friends," and the club servants. Irina's father, Lavr Mironych, who has often been imprisoned for debt, forms a pair with a club waiter, from whom he orders a gourmet supper for family and friends. While the father and the waiter arrange food and drink, the Romantic couple Dulchin and Irina conclude their engagement. The alternation of dialogue between the two materialists and the Romantic pair is reminiscent of the same alternation of contrasting couples—Mephistopheles with Martha, and Faust with Gretchen—who follow each other on stage as on a merry-go-round in the garden scene of Goethe's *Faust*. However, the whole panorama of a Moscow business world which has become much more sophisticated since Ostrovsky first depicted it thirty years earlier can be struck out without detriment to the play's action, as Maria Savina showed when she started the tradition of omitting Act III in her revival of *The Final Sacrifice* at the Alexandrinsky Theater in 1892.

The final twist of the surprise ending, for all its difference from the open endings of the early Ostrovsky plays, has one similarity with them: for Dulchin, at least, it means a return to the necessity he faced at the start, that of finding a rich widow to pay his debts. So, though in one sense an open ending, in another it is an action which has come full circle. The carrousel action which begins all over again at the end is frequent in the theater of the absurd, as in Samuel Beckett's *Waiting for Godot,* or Max Frisch's *Die Chinesische Mauer* (The Chinese Wall), and like all duplication tends to be comic. So the author's designation of the play as a comedy is justified to this extent.

For Julia, however, the comedy is somber. She has her heart set on Dulchin, of whose constant deception she is half aware: even on first entrance she tells of her foreboding that he may leave her.

Coming late from church because she stopped after the service to watch a wedding, she saw how "a girl came in and stood at a distance. There was not a drop of blood in her cheeks, her eyes burned, she fixed them on the groom and was all a-tremble, as if beside herself. Then I saw her starting to cross herself, and her tears flowed in streams. . . . And I myself wept" (Act I, Sc. 2; IV, 327). Julia has seen the counterpart of Dunya, Benevolensky's abandoned mistress, standing in the crowd at his wedding to the poor bride. Julia would have played much the same role had she gone to the engagement party for Dulchin and Irina.

Julia feels wholly certain of Dulchin except for the one moment just before he dashes her hopes for good, the moment when she decides on her dress and a bouquet of forget-me-nots for the wedding he has promised her. Even so, she praises her own good business sense in requiring his IOU for every penny she has lent him, and also for lending against the security of his estate, which she does not know is gone. And it is not the news of his engagement which prostrates her: for this she only wants, as she says, "to look him in the eyes" (Act IV, Sc. 9; IV, 395). Instead she succumbs to fainting and delirium when she learns that his notes are without security. Apparently she consents to marry Pribytkov because that experienced businessman will accept the task of recovering her fortune from Dulchin. Thus Julia, who gives all her love—all her money—returns in order to recover it. Of course her fear of having made a fool of herself may also lend her the will to strike back.

Pribytkov, like Berkutov in *Wolves and Sheep*, undertakes his fiancée's financial rescue. Yet he is unlike Ostrovsky's other business men in that he is second-generation wealthy. He wears no beard (earlier the hallmark of a class known as "the beards"), nor need he acquire wealth. He already possesses it, along with such cultural interests as a taste for theater, to which in Act I he tries to convert Julia.

The least credible character in the play is Dulchin. More precisely, it is incredible that three women should compete to be despoiled by so selfish and transparent a wastrel. An aristocrat exhibiting the evidently beguiling manners of the upper class, he is capable of running through a fortune, his own and anyone else's, while giving nothing in return but his charm. Neither his nor Julia's marriage is motivated by love, but by expediency and hard financial necessity.

The minor characters in the play are also moved by the same fiscal mainspring. A unique figure is Dulchin's usurer Salay Saltanych. Dergachev, Dulchin's friend and go-between—he must deceive Julia about the latter's absences—emulates his superior by asking for a ruble every time Dulchin asks for thousands. As handyman to Dulchin, who would mend his fortunes by marriage, he is reminiscent of Rasplyuev, helper to the hero in a similar situation in Alexander Sukhovo-Kobylin's classic comedy *The Marriage of Krechinsky*, which Meyerhold called "the tragedy of people concerned with money, connected with money for the sake of money, in the name of money."[2] That pronouncement on Sukhovo-Kobylin's comedy could apply just as well to *The Final Sacrifice*.

Yet the Moscow business people of this play differ decisively from those of Ostrovsky's first play of some thirty years before. Pribytkov by recommending to Julia the internationally famous Italian tragic actor Ernesto Rossi, or Irina's father in ordering a gourmet dinner for his guests display European sophistication. Irina's businessman father, Lavr Mironych, is evidently as much of a spendthrift as the aristocrat Dulchin, and can boast of having often been in debtor's prison, with which Dulchin is merely threatened. By the late 1870s the Moscow businessman Pribytkov is the equal of wheeler-dealer aristocrats like Vasilkov *(Easy Money)* and Berkutov *(Wolves and Sheep)*, and his nephew Lavr Mironych, of ruined aristocrats like Telyatev *(Easy Money)* and Dulchin. The hierarchy of *samodurstvo* has been replaced by an egalitarian sliding scale calibrated in rubles.

The actress Maria Savina dramatically challenged the new social status of Beyond-the-River Moscow when at first she refused the role of Julia, saying "she could not play these parts with shawls [over their heads]."[3] Ostrovsky had to explain that she did not wear a shawl at all. Rather, he said, "such businessmen's wives as Tugina dress much better and more expensively than aristocratic ladies."[4] Evidently Savina did then play Julia with shattering effectiveness, especially in the fourth act, just as Alexander Lensky at the Moscow premiere made Dulchin's charm believable. When Savina revived the play fifteen years later, she played Julia with new mastery, according to the critic Peter Gnedich, who thought her too young for the role when she first played it.[5]

Though not among Ostrovsky's most popular plays, *The Final Sacrifice* has remained, like *Wolves and Sheep*, among Ostrovsky's more often produced ones. To modern audiences it must seem a somber period piece. True, social relations can be founded upon wealth now just as they were then. But women today need not suffer

shipwreck any more than men on the rocks of expedience, nor find
rescue only in marriage.

II   *Give Me Love or Give Me Death:* Fiancée without Fortune
(1879)

For strictly business reasons Julia in *The Final Sacrifice* must
make a loveless match so as to recoup her financial losses. Larisa
Ogudalova, the heroine of *Bespridannitsa* (Fiancée without Fortune, literally the girl without a dowry, 1879), who lacks fortune,
loses security in marriage, and even life itself for love.

At the start of this "drama in four acts" Larisa intends to break
with her frivolous past and find financial security by marrying a
petty official, Karandyshev. Simultaneously, the indigent aristocrat
Paratov, her former lover and the light of her earlier social life,
reappears. Despite Larisa's pleas, her fiancé, Karandyshev, insists
on celebrating their engagement with a party, to which he invites
Paratov. Though Larisa believes she has reconciled the two, Paratov
has in fact sworn to humiliate his rival, and connives with his
near-alcoholic henchman, Arkady Schastlivtsev, to get Karandyshev
drunk. Overweening in his drunkenness, Karandyshev forbids
Larisa to sing for the guests. Though she herself had meant to
refuse, his assertion of authority goads her to accept. Carried away
by the gypsy mood of the song, the guests take Larisa with them for
a last party on Paratov's steamer, which he will be forced for lack of
funds to sell on the morrow. When Karandyshev misses her, he
snatches up a pistol and sets off to find her.

The next morning Larisa expects Paratov to marry her, but he
then tells her what everyone else has known since his return: he is
engaged to an heiress. When Karandyshev finds Larisa then, she
provokes him into shooting her.

Like his contemporaries, the great Russian Realists Dostoevsky,
Tolstoy, and Turgenev, who utilized reportage from newspapers or
actual encounters as inspiration for their novels, Ostrovsky based his
play on the case of a girl murdered by a jealous lover in Kineshma
near his summer home which had come before him in his capacity as
judge of civil court. Under financial pressure at this time of his life to
turn out a play a year, he devoted four years of careful work to this
one, perhaps because it was a milestone: when it was completed in
October 1878, he could mark it Opus 40.

The setting, reminiscent of that of *The Storm* in the fictive Volga town of Kalinov, is "the present in the large city of Bryakhimov on the Volga. The town promenade on a high bank of the Volga . . ., upstage a low iron grille, beyond it a view of the Volga, of a large panorama: forests, villages, and so on . . ." (Initial stage direction, PSS 12, V, 8).[6]

The three unities are admirably observed in the play. The time of the action is twenty-four hours, and the place Bryakhimov, though from the high promenade of Acts I and IV the action moves indoors to Larisa's in Act II, and Karandyshev's in Act III. Prehistory important for the play's action is provided through an extended exposition, first between two waiters at the café on the high promenade, then between the two rich businessmen, Knurov and Vozhevatov. The action may be called "analytic," as in Henrik Ibsen's Ghosts: that is, essential data, literally "given" to start with, release an action coiled like a spring for the final thrust, which constitutes the course of the play on stage.

Larisa's first speeches in the play announcing her resolve to embark on a new course—"You see, I am at the crossroads" (Act I, Sc. 4; V, 21), she tells Karandyshev—are belied by the cannon salute to Paratov's steamer, the Swallow. His return launches the action on the last lap of the old course. Karandyshev's jealous questions demonstrate the depth of his rivalry with Paratov. Larisa's story of Paratov's marksmanship spurs the office clerk to emulate the dashing aristocrat. "He's an ideal of a man" (Act I, Sc. 4; V, 22), Larisa says, and recalls an occasion when an officer, on a challenge from Paratov, shot a glass of water from the latter's head. But because Paratov saw the officer turn pale at the risk, Paratov repeated the challenge: asking Larisa to hold a coin between her fingers, he shoots it from her hand without blenching. Thus Larisa idealizes her view of Paratov as epigone of Pushkin's Romantic hero Silvio in "The Shot." Certainly Paratov treats Larisa rather as Pechorin, Mikhail Lermontov's antihero of that earlier time, deals with his women. Ostrovsky evidently thought the Romantic hero outmoded by that time, for he wrote his collaborator Nikolay Solovev that "our Pechorins are wearing out the ideals of the 1840s."[7] Still, Larisa's story not only reflects the aspirations of the three principals in the triangle at the core of the action, but also provides a justification for the incongruous display of weapons on the petty official's wall, from which Karandyshev then takes the fatal gun.

A heroine who idealizes a Romantic hero was not the Larisa

played by Vera Komissarzhevskaya in her performance at St. Petersburg's Alexandrinsky Theater, in 1897. Rather she saw in her an Everywoman who had failed to find a place in the world: as Larisa says, "I looked for love, and did not find it" (Act IV, Sc. 11; V, 81). Komissarzhevskaya replaced a song by the poet Eugene Baratynsky which Larisa sings in Act III, with a gypsy song ending "No, he did not love me." As the actor Yury Yurev describes her rendering of the song, she ended it "with such a crescendo, such a cry of the soul, as if her heart had burst."[8] The influential theater critic Alexander Kugel called to a colleague at intermission: "You are right when you say of her emphases that they do no wholly correspond to Ostrovsky's. . . . His colors are to be applied in broad strokes with the brush of [the Russian painter Ilya] Repin! But this is watercolor . . . done in blood."[9] So Komissarzhevskaya made dominant a single and obvious dimension of the character: the melancholy, misunderstood Larisa.

Yet Ostrovsky undoubtedly meant Larisa to be quite complex, for he wrote the part for Maria Savina, an actress noted for her transitions from seeming coldness to sudden passion. So Larisa leaves on the spur of the moment at the end of Act III for the night boat party, though she has just vowed never to be deceived again, that is if she was speaking for herself in the song she had just sung, the gypsy version of a Glinka composition to words by Pushkin's contemporary Eugene Baratynsky:

> Do not tempt me unless you must
> With renewal of your affection.
> To one disappointed in love
> All the former lures are alien.
>
> I don't believe assurances,
> No longer believe in love,
> And will not again fall prey
> To the dreams which once deceived me.
> (Act III, Sc. 11; V, 60)

One word from Paratov, however, suffices to overcome the disillusionment she has expressed in the song. Larisa goes with him again, when, applauding her, he says: "A few more such minutes . . . and I shall throw all calculation to the winds, no force will take you from me, unless it takes my life as well" (Act III, Sc. 12; V, 62). When the dispute between them continues the next morning, in

disillusionment Larisa upbraids Paratov with the words of another
Romantic poet, Lermontov:

> The light in his eyes
> Is bright as the skies. . . .
>
> (Act IV, Sc. 7; V, 76)

She does not speak the lines with which Lermontov's poem "To the
portrait" continues:

> In his soul all
> Is dark as the sea!

Although Larisa is a Romantic, both Paratov and she, the only
aristocrats in the play, are subject to the bourgeois business pres-
sures of the times, and Paratov capitulates to them. He has returned
to sell his boat to the businessman Vozhevatov. When Knurov asks
whether he is sorry to have to do this, he replies: "What do you
mean 'sorry'; I don't know anything of the sort. I hold nothing
sacred. . . . If I find it advantageous, I'll sell anything it suits me to
sell" (Act I, Sc. 6; V, 26). He explains to Larisa's mother that by
marrying a rich girl he is selling his own freedom, that is, selling
himself in marriage. No wonder he shows no regret at selling Larisa,
so to speak, down the river.

Paratov warns his actor-henchman Robinzon—the only other
significant character who is also not of the bourgeois class—that the
age of business has begun: "Adapt to circumstances, my poor friend.
The time of the Maecenas is gone; nowadays the business class is in
the ascendancy" (Act IV, Sc. 7; V, 73–74).

Larisa also displays an aristocratic disdain toward her devotee
Karandyshev when he finds her on the morning after the boat party.
Seated at the café table, and catching sight of him as she raises her
head she says:

How repulsive you are to me, if only you knew! Why are you here?
Karandyshev: Where am I supposed to be?
Larisa: I don't know. Wherever you want, only not where I am." (Act IV,
Sc. 11; V, 79)

So begins the interview in which she goads him into shooting her. In
the final accounting Larisa will not compromise her sensibility for

the sake of subsistence in the age of business, however she might have meant to do so for a while.

Larisa remains steadfast in her rejection of the business ethic, though both Knurov and Vozhevatov watch the market, hoping to buy her at the right moment as a mistress to take on a trip to Paris. The younger Vozhevatov yields her to the older Knurov not only because the latter can pay more, but also because he has won her by the flip of a coin. Karandyshev tells Larisa:

They regard you, not as a woman, not as a human being—a human being determines his own fate; they regard you as a thing. . . .
Larisa (deeply offended): A thing . . . yes, a thing! . . . (Heatedly) At last the right word for me. . . . (Act IV, Sc. 11; V, 79–80)

Then Karandyshev, adding insult to injury, tells her he owns her. And just as violently as Katherine rejected the tyranny of *samodurstvo* in *The Storm*, Larisa now refuses to be owned in the business age.

Larisa's end has been interpreted not as her declaration of freedom, but as her fiancé's jealous revenge. In three speeches before Karandyshev kills her she pretends that she is going away with Knurov, even though she has already unambiguously refused Knurov's offer. Her remark to Karandyshev is thus sheer provocation: "I did not find love, so I shall seek gold" (Act IV, Sc. 11; V, 81). (Paratov, by the way, has found gold with a fiancée whose wealth derives from gold mines.) Larisa now wants only to die, and at once changes her tone as soon as Karandyshev has fired. She thanks him, and draws the pistol toward herself, whispering that the blame is hers. The shot through which he means to assert ownership—"Not mine!" he cries; "Then you shall not belong to anyone!" (ibid.; V, 81)—actually sets her free. She falls facing him, not turning to go with Knurov.[10]

Like Katherine with her query "Why can't people fly?" Larisa from the start has looked into the distance seeking freedom: for instance, upon her first entrance she sits looking at the view through binoculars before speaking. Even her name, related to the Greek for "sea gull," alludes to flight. She has not sold herself, unlike Paratov, who seven times in half as many speeches refers to his chains, the last time when he shows her his engagement ring: "Here are the golden chains which bind me for my whole life" (Act IV, Sc. 7; V, 76).

Knurov and Vozhevatov represent the business ethic which Paratov has accepted. Vozhevatov, who is buying the "Swallow," makes it clear that he could pay for a trip to Paris with Larisa as his mistress from the profit on the resale of the boat. In the same breath, as if referring to Larisa, he remarks: "Every piece of merchandise has its price" (Act I, Sc. 2; V, 14). Both consider love bad for business, and have no morals that money will not override. Thus Knurov, when he promises Larisa to fulfill her every wish if she will go with him, tells her: "I can offer you such an enormous stipend that even the most wicked critics of other people's morals must fall silent . . ." (Act IV, Sc. 8; V, 77). These two are no longer Moscow merchants but big businessmen on a European scale, drinking champagne instead of tea and taking their pleasure in Paris.

While the businessmen of this late play have come up in the world, the actor Arkady Schastlivtsev has fallen to the status of a drunken jester nicknamed Robinzon, a man to be exploited and also put off, since his only aim in life is to drink himself into insensibility. The play's other Bohemians, the gypsies, at least earn their drink by their music, and one of their number, Ilya, who accompanies Larisa on the guitar, sings the tenor voice of her song in Act III, thus aligning her with them.

This, then, is a drama of free spirits whose freedom has ended in an age of big business. The swift movement of the single-line action within the three unities, the lyric core in the disillusionment of the Baratynsky elegy, the background of gypsy music, and above all the appeal of a heroine now disillusioned, now passionate, who in the end rejects the material blandishments of her pursuers, all these things have made *Fiancée without Fortune* one of Ostrovsky's best plays, and led to its adaptation as ballet, film, and opera.

III   *Life of the Heart or in Art?* Career Woman *(1882)*

If Larisa cannot marry for love as she would like, Alexandra Nikolaevna Negina, the heroine of *Talanty i poklonniki*, (Career Woman, literally Talents and Admirers, 1882), will not marry for love of her art. If Larisa refuses to sell herself without love to her admirers, Negina rejects her true love and sells herself to an admirer so as to continue with her art. Finally, if Larisa, raised in the genteel tradition, has no work and hence no way of supporting herself, Negina is the only kind of working woman Ostrovsky knows: an actress.

The actress's mother, Domna Pantelevna, who had enough of precarious living with her dead husband, a musician in a provincial theater orchestra, urges her daughter to accept a wealthy suitor and leave the theater for security's sake. Negina, however, rejects this counsel both because her elderly coach Narokov believes in her talent, and because she is engaged to the poor student Peter Meluzov. Meluzov arms her with a moral sensitivity which leads her to refuse to become the mistress of Prince Dulebov.

In revenge for that rebuff, Dulebov persuades her manager Migaev not to renew her contract. However, the estate owner Velikatov, an admirer of the actress Smelskaya, buys out the house for Negina's last benefit performance, and resells the tickets at a profit, even providing one for a high price to Dulebov. On the benefit evening Negina receives two letters: one is from her Petya asking her to meet him after the show; the other is from Velikatov, who asks her to be his mistress and promises to keep a theater always at her disposal. With Petya's help Negina ejects an over-weening admirer, Bakin, from her dressing room, and spends the night after the show in a last wild drive with Petya.

The next morning all have gathered at the railroad station to see Negina and her mother off to Moscow. Narokov, who has pawned his last possession for champagne, toasts the actress's talent, and for the sake of that talent she says goodby to Petya. Velikatov, who has provided a special car for the travelers, to everyone's surprise goes away with the actress. Still, Negina and Petia part amicably, as each continues in devotion to his own: Negina to her acting, Petya to his teaching.

As first conceived at the end of the summer of 1881, this "comedy in four acts" was to have been about a stage-struck actress, and the first draft bore the title "Dreamers" [*Mechtateli*]. Narokov brings out the dream theme in Act I as a defense against Domna Pan-televna's contempt for the failure and poverty it has brought him. He repeats it in Act IV in his toast to the departing Negina: "And have faith, / Not vain are the poet's dreams" (Act IV, Sc. 6; V, 274). These are the dreams which Negina too chooses by devoting her life to the theater. But Petya also dreams of high ideals.

At their first encounter Velikatov defines the difference between Petya's dreams and his own practical way of life:

Such noble, elevated goals. . . . It's really enviable.
Meluzov: What's so enviable? What's to prevent your having noble, elevated goals?
Velikatov: No, that's not for us, I beg you. The prose of life has us in its
grip. . . . Practical considerations, material calculations. . . . One always
has to do with the sphere of the possible, the attainable. . . .
Meluzov: And what do you call noble, elevated goals?
Velikatov: Why, goals in which there's a great deal of nobility, and very
little chance of success. (Act I, Sc. 9; V, 229)

Petya gives Negina lessons, if not in the dreams to which she
naturally aspires, then in his higher morality. To be sure, she is
plagued by practical considerations:

Negina: Oh dear, I don't need lessons, but money.
Meluzov: I too am short on that. . . . But, come Sasha, let's have our
confession. . . . See, you tell me what you felt, said, and did; and I'll tell
you how you should feel, speak, and act. So you'll gradually improve, and
in time you'll be . . .
Negina: What shall I be, my dear?
Meluzov: You'll be a thoroughly good woman. (Act I, Sc. 11; V, 231)

In the final accounting neither Petya's principles nor the thunder of
artistic ideals, expressed, as in *The Forest*, by the tragedian, avail
against the manager's cabal: only Velikatov's practical measures
help.

When in the end Negina realizes that an actress must be a heroine
to be a "good woman" and renounces Petya's ideals, Petya does not
give up. This time he argues not against practicality, but against the
immorality of Bakin, one of the wealthy set who prey on the
Bohemian theater world, seeking to exploit the actresses sexually.
Petya gives affirmative answers to Bakin's questions: "Teach again?
. . . And again an actress? . . . And you'll fall in love again, dream
again. . . ?" (Act IV, Sc. 9; V, 279).

Meluzov goes on to describe his world of dreams, so different
from Negina's: he longs for the progress of science and the advance
of civilization. It is true that he has fallen into rather the wrong
world, that of actresses and their admirers: "But I penetrated, so to
speak, into an alien realm, into a land of happy sojourn, carefree
pastime, into a sphere of beautiful, gay women, a sphere of champagne, bouquets, expensive gifts . . ." (ibid.) In speaking to Bakin,

who belongs in this other world, Petya sums it up thus: "I enlighten [people], and you corrupt [them]" (ibid.). Yet these two also part amicably. Dramatic conflict is as absent from their encounter as it is from the meeting of Petya and Velikatov. Negina's and Petya's dreams do not conflict either.

Ostrovsky was quite right to change the play's initial title to the present one, which promises a portrayal of theater life on both sides of the footlights. Though the play is formally set in Bryakhimov on the Volga, the city and its situation are this time immaterial to the action, for the play actually takes place in the world of the provincial theater.

The characters cannot be divided in the same way as in the early plays into exploiters and exploited, though the admirers, except for Meluzov, exploit the actresses sexually, and are in return themselves exploited for gifts and other gains. Thus the scene is the Bohemian life of the theater, which Negina chooses not to leave. In so doing she rejects Meluzov's morality, for certainly Velikatov has no more intention of marrying her than did Dulebov.

The panorama of theater life is of greater interest than the characters, which are not depicted in great depth. Some of the secondary figures are characterized by Dickension leitmotifs. Thus the drunken tragic actor repeats at each appearance, "Where is my Vasya?", summoning his admirer and patron to bring him the drink to which he is addicted. Though he tries to storm at the manager in Negina's defence, his inebriated ineffectuality invites only unfavorable comparison with the tragedian Neschastlivtsev of *The Forest*.

Negina's preceptor in the arts Narokov, who sets the ominous precedent of having given all for the theater, pronounces at every setback his amusingly melodramatic leitmotif signature. "[Plunge] the dagger to the hilt into my breast!" (see, for example, Act II, Sc. 2; V, 237).

Domna Pantelevna, too, has her repeated character tag, the malapropism or comic speech error. Thus Narokov has to correct her when she calls him a "chou-fleur" [cauliflower] instead of "souffleur" [prompter], the name of the low theatrical post to which he has fallen (Act I, Sc. 2; V, 213). Not only does Domna by her presence show whence Negina has come, she also influences her daughter's choice of financial security in the end. Paradoxically as a parent she does not necessarily argue for morality. Thus, though she at first favors Meluzov because he proposes marriage, she scolds her

daughter for offending Dulebov by rejecting less than that. Velikatov wins her support not only by giving her a shawl as a gift, but
also by describing the poultry on his estate where they will live if
Negina goes with him. Domna is a bird fancier who also has a
dream: one of pure white swans, if only her daughter will accept
Velikatov.

The daughter Negina was central to the play from the start, as
Ostrovsky described his early idea for it: "An actress who has
devoted her life to the stage from childhood appears; theater types,
her struggle, and her ruin."[11] Apparently Ostrovsky felt some
affinity with his heroine, for she was the only figure in all his work
upon whom he bestowed his own first name and patronymic,
Alexandra Nikolaevna. Yet he has her give herself to her fiancé
without meaning to marry him, as well as become Velikatov's
mistress for material reasons. On the other hand, she is not the
shallow Bohemian without a conscience that is Smelskaya, her
fellow actress and friend, who accepts without scruple everything
her admirers offer.

After Negina's indignant rejection of Dulebov and Petya's instruc-
tions in morality, her departure with Velikatov comes as the surprise of the fourth act. No monologue "to be or not to be" fills the
hiatus between the last two acts, or reveals her state of mind
between her surrender to Petya and her farewell the next day. The
scene merely shifts, and with it the point of view, from Negina
herself to the admirers waiting to see her off. The audience is then
confronted with the decision which she had not intended to explain
even to Petya, whom she had asked not to come to the station—
thence she was supposed to leave for a new job in Moscow, not for
the South with Velikatov. This gap may explain why the critic
Aleksey Suvorin commented that the play "does not exhaust the
content of its theme,"[12] and called it simply "a series of scenes."[13]

With Negina's conflict of conscience left so open to interpretation,
critics have arrived at different readings of her character. The actor
Yury Yurev cites her feeling that to ride away with Meluzov that
night is good and honest, in order to comment paradoxically: "Here
is a pure impulse of the soul, pure even in its fall."[14] He goes on to
term her second fall with Velikatov a heroic self-sacrifice for the sake
of her calling. The Soviet scholar Vladimir Lakshin decreases the
importance of her choice by asserting Negina did not really care for
Meluzov,[15] but then it was indeed immoral for her to spend the

night with him. Lakshin also simplifies her career choice by assuming that she is "a real talent."[16] But surely at this point in her career her talent is yet to be proved. Still, she is certain of her calling, for she tells Meluzov: "I am an actress. . . . If I married you, I would soon leave you, and go on the stage; even for a pittance salary, just to be on the stage. Do you think I can live without theater?" (Act IV, Sc. 7; V, 276).

Meluzov had to be deceived into thinking his Sasha would marry him, though, for otherwise he could not have gone off with her after the benefit. Afterwards he condemns her conduct as "depravity," but doubtless only because he is quoting from Pushkin's little tragedy *Mozart and Salieri:* "Could it be that talent and depravity are indissolubly linked?" (Act IV, Sc. 7; V, 276). Actually even Meluzov can adjust, as when he writes Negina: "Yes, dear Sasha, art is not nonsense, I'm beginning to understand that" (Act III, Sc. 7; V, 263).

In a production of the play in 1969 the Mayakovsky Theater in Moscow, made Petya a rough and ready, much abused hero. In criticizing the production, Efim Kholodov was displeased that Petya was the sort to arouse the audience's sympathy and Velikatov was debased to a near-villain of a prosy businessman. In fact Velikatov is a good estate and factory manager, quite close in many ways to Berkutov, and a retired cavalry officer, related to the dashing Paratov. His shyness and confession of loneliness to Negina's mother give him some of Vasilkov's appeal. On the whole, though, he is perhaps the least clearly realized character in the play.

Astonishingly, Ostrovsky gives the play's final speech to a person not of the theater, Meluzov, who again declares his undying faith in his teaching profession, "in the possibility of improving people" (Act IV, Sc. 9; V, 280). But this was also Ostrovsky's credo for the theater, and it is to art and the theater that he gives the moral victory in this, his best portrayal of theater life.

The opening of *Career Woman* in Moscow was performed by a memorable cast with Ermolova in the lead; that in Saint Petersburg with Savina represented a personal triumph for the author, who was called out for applause at the end of each act after the first. The play has been only moderately popular in the USSR, though, however much it may speak to modern women in the West. In 1956 A. Apsolon and Boris Dmokhovsky directed a motion picture of it for Lenfilm.

IV   *Mother's Day:* Guilty without Guilt *(1844)*

The heroine of *Bez viny vinovatye* (Guilty without Guilt, 1884)
speaks for a social cause, that of unwed mothers and illegimate
children, as well as for several other heroines of Ostrovsky's when
she says: "I know that there is a great deal of nobility, love,
self-sacrifice in people, especially in women" (Act II, Sc.
4; V, 382).
If not all of Ostrovsky's self-sacrificing females have been wholly
unselfish, at least Kruchinina in this play seems so. She is,
moreover, an actress devoted to her calling, and an older woman,
even a mother.

The seamstress Otradina, who has had to place her child by
Murov in foster care until he keeps his promise to marry her, learns
that he is marrying a girl with money instead. This blow is followed
by another when the foster nurse summons her to her child, who is
mortally ill.

Seventeen years later the great actress Kruchinina comes to the
same provincial city to appear with the local theater company. She
saves a young actor, Neznamov, from being arrested in a brawl he
has begun when taunted about his bastard origin. Kruchinina
confesses to the wealthy Dudukin that the humanity of her art
derives from her having lived through the death of her son years ago
in this very city, for she is the jilted and bereaved Otradina.

Though Neznamov, incited by his boon companion, the actor
Shmaga, ungratefully challenges Kruchinina for her intercession on
his behalf, she returns his rudeness with charity. The by now
half-demented old nurse comes to tell her that her son is not in fact
dead, as she had been led to believe.

Korinkina and Milovzorich, actors of the local troupe who envy
the guest star, denigrate her in Neznamov's eyes by repeating the
rumor that the great actress had once cruelly abandoned a child.

Kruchinina proudly rejects a marriage proposal from Murov,
demanding only to know where her son is. Murov has lost track of
him, but informs her that he had put her locket around the child's
neck. At Dudukin's reception for the actors Neznamov displays the
locket he wears in bitter reproach to Kruchinina, who faints from
shock upon recognizing it. But she soon recovers to embrace in
Neznamov the son she had mourned so long.

This "comedy in four acts" illustrates Efim Kholodov's observation that the beginnings of Ostrovsky's plays are just as open as their
conclusions. Kholodov decides that the author thus "washes over"

the start "in an effort to wipe away the borderline between what might have happened before the curtain rose, and what will happen before our eyes. The action is continuous."[17] Thus the curtain rises on *Guilty without Guilt* to reveal the seamstress Annie biting off a thread as she finishes a customer's wedding dress. As her fellow worker Otradina learns to her shock, the dress is for the other woman whom Murov is to wed. As Kholodov notes, such ongoing action requires the exposition of "prehistory" so frequent in the late plays. This play opens *in medias res*, actually in a prologue depicting events which precede the main action by almost two decades. So the audience first sees a prehistory, which in its turn requires an explanation, that is, a preprehistory.

As N. S. Grodskaya remarks in her article on the history of its origins,[18] the play has two basic themes: the heroine's maternal feelings, and her artistic calling. The two are intertwined, for the actress Kruchinina owes her greatness in projecting human feeling on stage to her experience of a mother's sorrow.

Unfortunately the two themes are conjoined in a plot which is complex in an outmoded and melodramatic way. Thus when Otradina hears of her son's illness, she rushes to his side, but faints upon finding him blue and gasping for breath. Her unmaternal reaction is explained, however: it seems she is herself ill with diphtheria, and so is spirited away to her grandmother's in the country for a month and a half. Murov's letter with the news of their son's death and burial is withheld from her until she recovers. Why she should then seek no verification of the news, and fail to visit the grave, is unclear: instead she continues to live with the grandmother in the Crimea, and travels with her abroad. After inheriting a comfortable sum upon her grandmother's death, she decides to become an actress.

Meantime, like the children exposed to die in ancient myth and medieval legend, her son is brought up by a childless couple ignorant of his identity. Only seventeen years later does the mother learn he is still alive; and then she finds him close at hand, still wearing the identifying token around his neck. Her fainting upon recognizing him again seems improbable in a woman with the stamina to lead the life of an actress on tour.

It is true that the plot of the foundling restored to his rightful heritage would have been very familiar to English readers of Henry Fielding's *Tom Jones,* or Charles Dickens's *Oliver Twist,* but Ostrovsky endows it with new meaning by making Kruchinina's loss of her child the source of her ability to show feeling on stage. Such a Stanislavskian view—and this years before Stanislavsky—of experience as the basis for the actor's art was expounded earlier by the actor hero of *The Forest*, Neshchastlivtsev, in trying to recruit Aksyusha for the theater: "You know storms, know passions—and that's enough," the tragic actor tells her, as if the despair manifested in her suicide attempt were sufficient qualification for an actress (*The Forest*, Act IV, Sc. 6; III, 313). So the melodramatic coincidences of Kruchinina's loss and recovery of her child become the experience essential to Kruchinina's deep artistic humanity.

Of the two interconnected themes, the first is emphasized in the title, with its thrust against the injustices suffered by both unwed mother and child. The local patron of the arts Dudukin explains to Kruchinina how Neznamov's lack of status has made him a rebellious nature: "He became an angry young man, and wild to the point of biting like an animal" (Act II, Sc. 3; V, 373). He had even been sent as a settler to Siberia because he lacked a passport, and hence can easily be returned there upon the slightest difficulty, such as the brawl after which Kruchinina intercedes for him. Dudukin prepares her for his unruly temper, his drinking with Shmaga, and his quarrelsome conduct: "You imagine [as your son] a smiling little angel face with blond, silky curls. . . . And suddenly a disheveled rowdy reels in, like Neznamov, unshaven, smelling of cheap cigarettes and booze" (Act II, Sc. 3; V, 377).

Kruchinina, though, seems untouched by cruel reality. She twice wins the young man over. The first time—when Shmaga and he come to challenge her for her kindness—she not only pays their bill at the bar, but also gives Neznamov a ten-ruble tip, and enough more to buy Shmaga an overcoat. Doubtless inspired by "the voice of the blood," as the melodramatic cliché has it, she then embraces the young actor. When he is incited by the envious Korinkina and Milovzorich to challenge her again, she is overcome by emotion upon recognizing him.

Kruchinina's excess of feeling is clearly genuine, not artificial, as the two conspirators had led Neznamov to suspect. The Soviet critic Lakshin finds that in Kruchinina Ostrovsky has further developed a theme frequent in his work—the betrayal of a loving heart—and shown for once how a heroine who survives the blow may carry on. But Lakshin also observes: "The spectator is shown. . . . Kruchinina's talent, her success, and her theatrical renown as a *fait accompli*. He must take the playwright's word for it that she has achieved all that herself, whereas the action has concentrated on the melodramatic story of the mother's recovery of the son she thought dead."[19] Her assumption that Neznamov too can become a fine actor and a good person once he has found his mother, must also be taken on faith.

To only one person does Kruchinina show herself unfeeling, though justifiably: she refuses to marry Murov in the end, preferring to retain both her profession and her son for herself. As she says to Neznamov in her penultimate lines: "What do you need a father for? You will be a good actor, and we have some capital. As for a last name, . . . you will take mine" (Act IV, Sc. 10; V, 424).

So both mother and son remain true to the life of the theater, even more fully depicted in this than in Ostrovsky's other theater play, *Career Woman*. That picture is, on the one hand, not pretty: it includes unlovely sex relationships, professional jealousy, drinking and brawling accompanied even by arrests; the unbalanced economics whereby the star receives the lion's share of receipts; drafty, dingy, dressing rooms; and bourgeois disdain for this Bohemian world in which some, like Shmaga, have blemished records, and others, like Neznamov, none at all. On the other hand, the play also brings out the humanity and greatness of the actor's art at its best.

To emphasize the theater life shown in the play, the 1930 production by the Studio of the Maly Theater omitted its first act; the Maly director F. N. Kaverin meant thereby also to eliminate the melodramatic situation of unwed mother and dying child.[20] Though this very situation (when Otradina tells her faithless lover he is free of any obligation to her now that their child is at death's door) had left not a dry eye among nineteenth-century audiences, it must seem exaggerated in our time, for the first act is frequently omitted today. Thus the play's leading role is that of an older woman, and *Guilty without Guilt* becomes a drama lacking a love affair and dealing instead with a mother-son relationship.

But then the interpretation of the production at Moscow's Pushkin Theater in 1978 devalued the mother-son relationship as well. Shaking his head "no," Neznamov retreats in the end from his mother's embrace, and departs with the dropout and rebel Shmaga instead. By so doing he strikes a blow not only against sentimentality, but also against the great theater art dear both to the author and his heroine.

Guilty without Guilt not only provides a starring role for older great actresses, but also continues to vie with *The Forest* for first place in popularity among Ostrovsky's plays; the humanity of its subject brought it to the fore especially in the war years. Grodskaya exaggerates, though, when she writes that it is "the last important work [by Ostrovsky] to become part of the golden treasury of world drama."[21] Though undoubtedly an important play, and one unquestionably effective on stage, it is hardly even known in world literature, much less famous as one of its treasures.

V *The Unworldly Wife:* Not of This World *(1855)*

In contrast to the frequently performed *Guilty without Guilt*, Ostrovsky's last play, *Ne ot mira sego* (*Not of This World*, 1885, subtitled "Family Scenes[22] in Three Acts"), is among his ten least frequently performed.

The heroine, Xenia, and her younger sister, Kapitolina, have been brought up not for this world but for the next by their Puritan mother, Snafidina, who is deeply disturbed that her elder and favorite daughter should have married the worldling Kochuev. Indeed, Kochuev's attempt to introduce Xenia to the gay life of society has so shattered her health that doctors have sent her abroad to recover. She is cured, however, when Kochuev resolves to abandon his former life and spend time with her. She obtains money from her inheritance to buy an estate for their life together in the country, and to pay the debts from his previous dissipation.

Only for the love of Xenia, whom he wishes to shield from the knowledge of an affair now terminated, has Kochuev failed to present two last bills owed for gifts to an actress. These bills are pilfered from Kochuev's desk by Barbarisov, Kapitolina's scheming fiancé. He resents Snafidina's giving her favorite Xenia the money for the estate out of the fortune of which his future wife should inherit half equally with her sister. He puts the bills into Xenia's hands, thus shaking her newly restored faith in her husband and reversing her precarious recovery. Though Kochuev and Xenia again protest their love for each other, the wife dies in her husband's arms.

At least one critic of the time, Sergey Flerov, discerned the action underlying the events of the play. As he put it, the play's poetic theme was expressed "not so much in what happens, as in what is said and revealed of processes taking place in the soul."[23] Though Flerov therefore called the play "a dramatic poem," the conflict is no less dramatic for being internal. Again Ostrovsky's characters must choose between worldly and other-worldly considerations.

At first glance Xenia seems wholly unworldly: after all, the title refers to her. Even her name comes from the Greek root meaning "strange" or "alien"—to this world, of course. Yet she has not only fallen in love with the worldly Kochuev, she has also married him, and against her mother's will. Though as the play opens, he thinks she is returning to him because he has promised to change his life, her motive is actually a material one. An anonymous letter—the audience guesses that it is from Barbarisov—has defamed Kochuev by falsely asserting that he must pay back an enormous sum missing at the bank where he works or face imprisonment. So she has rushed to his rescue before an audit at the beginning of the month should reveal the deficiency, without heeding the letter's exhortation: "Don't trust your husband; protect yourself and your fortune! Leave your money in the hands of your mother!" (Act I, Sc. 9; V, 440).

In reaching out to her husband's world, Xenia upon her arrival displays the quite feminine and mundane concern that he may find her weary and tousled from the journey. Kochuev's friend Elokhov tells her not to worry: "After all, he doesn't love you for your beauty" (Act I, Sc. 9; V, 443).

Her inner beauty of soul is Xenia's great asset. It makes her quite invulnerable to Kochuev's efforts to educate her in the ways of his world. She judges the off-color jokes in the operettas to which he takes her from a standpoint of pure morality: "She fixed on me her unrelenting gaze," he tells Elokhov, "and keeps repeating, 'No, now say, is that good or not?' There was no avoiding it. 'No, I answer, it isn't good' " (Act I, Sc. 2; V, 430).

Xenia's values affect Kochuev at first negatively, later positively. In corresponding with her, he declares, "I feel that I am myself reborn. I am getting to be a better person" (Act I, Sc. 3; V, 432). So Xenia draws Kochuev away from his worldly pleasures, until by the end of the central second act they resolve together to lead a life of prayer, culture, and work as well as play.

Though his friend tries to persuade Xenia that Kochuev is sincere, his conversion could be regarded as by no means disinterested. Has he only pretended to renounce the world in order to gain access to his wife's money? When after their marriage Xenia reproached him for his worldly ways, as he reports: "My mother-in-law did not at once pay out all the money she had promised [to settle on] her daughter. 'The rest,' she said, (and this rest amounted to around a hundred thousand), 'is for a year from now, when I see that you are living in agreement' " (Act I, Sc. 3; V, 431). Undoubtedly it would be worth feigning compatibility for so much money.

Certainly Kochuev's failure to meet his wife upon her return shows he is still very much involved with the world he intends to leave for her sake. "I've already sent the carriage and my man to the station," he explains. "I should go to meet her myself, but I must absolutely be at the theater just for half an hour, if only to show myself to my friends. There's a new operetta right now. Besides, Xenia will probably come tomorrow" (Act I, Sc. 3; V, 433). Even now he does not express a wholly positive view of his marriage: "My whole misfortune was to have married a virtuous girl. That was a big mistake. . . . How [hard it is] to have before you at every moment a strict moral censor!" (ibid.; V, 429). To prove his conversion, Kochuev protests that he has changed irrevocably, and that he has bought edifying books, though he admits he does not have an easy time reading them. Is this, indeed, the beginning of true love and a new life?

To begin with, Kochuev admits he is as calculating an aspirant to his wife's inheritance as Barbarisov, who hypocritically courts Kapitolina for her prospective fortune alone. Indeed the girls' mother has given each an equal dowry, but by withdrawing from capital the amount Xenia needed to buy the estate without assigning a comparable sum to Kapitolina, she has caused Barbarisov's complaint: "To one daughter [their mother] is ready to give her soul, but the other is as if not her daughter. . . . Xenia married almost against her mother's will; she has no children, and now that she's ill, has she got much longer to live?" (Act I, Sc. 6; V, 436). Of course, upon Xenia's death the estate will go to Kochuev, and not revert to her mother.

While he cannot prevent the mother from favoring one daughter, Barbarisov does try to give her objective reasons for preferring him to Kochuev, to which end he works hard and practices Puritan self-denial. He also writes unsigned letters to Xenia and steals Kochuev's unpaid bills, so as to blacken his rival in the eyes of the latter's wife and mother-in-law. And he does this in the name of justice, self-righteously declaring: "Vice should be punished. . . . But we see the opposite. . . . I'm that kind of person: injustice distresses me. I want everyone to receive according to his deserts" (Act I, Sc. 6; V, 436–37).

Snafidina, too, however much she indulges Xenia, does not want Kochuev to be the beneficiary of her wealth. The last of the *samodurs*, she wishes to decide the matter herself, even though Xenia should will the estate to her husband. The mother threatens to take any such will to court, then to a higher court, then to the Senate, and finally to take the law into her own hands if need be. "Oh, be quiet," she says to Barbarisov.

[You tell me] "The Senate will refuse you!" Now, what's that worth? I shall go higher. I ask you, what kind of law is that! There's only one law: "that children should obey their parents." And there are no other laws beside that. But if there are, I don't want to know them. Let whoever wants to, carry them out. I have no intention of doing so. I shall appeal that the courts be prohibited from arousing my daughters against me, so that their disobedience is not confirmed by the courts, and supported by some kind of laws of theirs. No, it's hard to argue with me; I, sir, am a mother. I know my rights; I must answer for my daughters in the other world. (Act II, Sc. 4; V, 453)

This widowed mother of two marriageable daughters, unlike Kukushkina in *A Profitable Post*, displays an other-worldly *samodurstvo*. Indeed, it is she who has brought up Xenia in other-worldliness, and she expresses her love for her thus: "Yes, truly, I love her very much; I loved her even as a child more than words can say. I begged, I prayed for her to die . . . to die in adolescence a virgin. Then she would have gone straight to the other world in all her youthful innocence" (Act II, Sc. 4; V, 456).

Though again money and schemes to obtain it motivate the plot on a material level, and though the subject of religious otherworldliness opposes and conjoins with it on a higher level, neither gives the play its theme, which is unique in the Ostrovsky canon and still relevant today. That theme could be summarily brushed aside as that age-old cliché "the double standard," but actually it is still a pressing problem: how can a woman share with a beloved partner a life as active and interesting as his in the world, and not be relegated to an observation deck?

In each of the first two acts Xenia reaches out to her husband in his world: in the first to rescue him in his supposed financial distress, in the second to embark with him on their new life together on the estate. Finally, however, she dies because the two cannot truly share their existence.

Xenia's unnamed illness is apparently not physical, but psychic.

As her husband describes it to Elokhov in Act I, when Kochuev asked forgiveness for his affairs with actresses, "she forgave me. Then for some reason she began feeling unwell, and then she became even quite ill; she was nervously altogether disturbed. . . . The doctors sent her abroad" (Act I, Sc. 3; V, 431). Kochuev makes it clear that her illness derived not from jealousy, but from moral revulsion at his unworthy preoccupations.

Despite their resolve at the turning point of their embrace in Act II, husband and wife cannot live alone apart from society. Though the ineluctably innocent woman fears Kochuev's friend Murugov, just as Gretchen instinctively dislikes Faust's worldly companion Mephistopheles—"I feel, . . ." Xenia says, "that he's come for my soul" (Act III, Sc. 4; V, 465)—Murugov is right. He ridicules a lawyer's wife who aspires to share her husband's life: "She cannot be without her husband even a few minutes, and is very sad that her husband does not take her with him to sit on the bench in civil court. 'I wouldn't be in anyone's way,' she says . . ." (Act III, Sc. 5; V, 467).

When Xenia dies, then, it is not so much because of the two bills which exposed an affair her husband had broken off, as because she has had to face the inevitable duality of their two worlds. As she says after Murugov has left: "We sensitive women, strange to the world, aren't fit for life on earth, and shouldn't live . . . [my husband] is afraid to offend me with my ignorance; he's afraid I will dispute indisputable realities, so he hides them, conceals them from me . . ." (Act III, Sc. 7; V, 469).

Such heroines as Katherine in *The Storm* and Larisa in *Fiancée without Fortune* found it difficult to depart from the all too real world, but Xenia simply "passes away." That euphemistic expression well describes the manner of her going, before Kochuev's assurances of love can save her. The factual mind finds it hard to believe in the existence of so psychic an illness, much less that it could culminate in death. Yet heroines who pine thus, even pine and die, are found elsewhere in nineteenth-century literature. Thus Adueva in Ivan Goncharov's *Ordinary Story* falls ill as a result of her husband's increasing worldly success and consequent neglect of her, until he finally resigns his high office and takes up a simple life in the country with her. Or again, Milly Teal in Henry James's *Wings of the Dove* turns her face to the wall to die when she learns that Densher, whom she loves, had meant to use her for worldly gain.

The mechanism by which so touching and significant a theme

finds expression in *Not of This World* is undoubtedly melodramatic, and the monologues which serve as exposition and confession are admittedly monotonous. That Elokhov should be simultaneously the confidant of Kochuev, Xenia's friend and adviser, and Snafidina's and Barbarisov's interlocutor, is as improbable as that Kochuev's living room should be the scene of Snafidina's council of war. It is unfortunate that the outworn machinery of a confidant and the unity of place should have to convey the subtle and interesting conflict between the real and ideal world in this marriage of true love.

Since it is so rarely performed, *Not of This World* seemed new and topical in a production directed by N. Dunaev for the Ostrovsky anniversary year of 1973 by the highly regarded Moscow Teatr na Maloi Bronnoi (Theater on Little Armorers' Street). Clearly the play is capable of moving a modern audience with the near abstraction of its setting and the perennial problem of its theme.

VI *Male Dove?* The Marriage of Belugin *(1878)*

Ostrovsky's undoubtedly most successful collaborative effort, *Zhenit'ba Belugina* (The Marriage of Belugin), was written with Nikolay Solovev. Except for *Vasilisa Melentieva* (1868), all the plays on which Ostrovsky collaborated with others, including four in all with Solovev, date from the last decade of his life, and exemplify both his willingness to help young dramatists and his interest in finding new writers for the Russian theater.

Solovev had capitulated to the poverty of life as a provincial schoolteacher by entering a monastery in 1874. There he showed two of his plays to a cell neighbor, Konstantin Leontev, the conservative critic and thinker. Leontev, fortuitously meeting Ostrovsky at Pisemsky's house in January 1876, then passed the manuscripts on to the master. Leontev recognized not only the young man's talent, but also his need for an apprenticeship in his craft. He wrote Solovev on April 9, 1876: "He [Ostrovsky] will help you perfect the form of your works, improve your stage devices, teach you not to use . . . seminarian's expressions [of which he gave examples]. . . ."[24] In the same letter Leontev warned his poorboy protégé, though, not to allow his ideas to be perverted by Ostrovsky's democratic and liberal attitudes.

Ostrovsky first freed Solovev from the monastery and helped him find employment. Then, inviting him to Shchelykovo, he reworked with him his play *Kto ozhidal* (Who Could Have Foreseen), which through two summers and four variants they transformed into the successful *The Marriage of Belugin*. Undoubtedly the master's hand was more important than the novice's to the finished play, of which Ostrovsky revised especially the last two acts.[25]

However, the critics, who tend to value the new more highly than the old; Leontev, who wished to keep his influence on the young man; and actors, notably Mikhail Sadovsky, who was then at odds[26] with Ostrovsky, all needled Solovev to liberate his supposedly greater gift from Ostrovsky's tutelage. Indeed, the latter moved from nearly abject gratitude at first to increasing resentment of his benefactor later, and Ostrovsky, as his would-be teacher, could only approve of his wish for independence. After a first success, though, Solovev alone wrote with diminishing acclaim, and none of his own plays has entered the classic repertory.

The action of the play has to do with what could be termed planned adultery. The plot of both *The Marriage of Belugin* and of Henry James's novel *The Wings of the Dove* hangs on a similar startling scheme: one of a pair of upper-class, luxury-addicted, but impoverished lovers will marry himself off to an unsophisticated, rich outsider, who will then unwittingly provide the money for the lovers to continue their affair in the expensive manner to which they are accustomed. However, the plan miscarries when the human sacrifice on the altar of the loveless marriage falls in love with his conjugal partner.

In Ostrovsky's play the sexes are paired differently than in James's novel, and the ending is a happy one, not tragic, as with James. The wealthy victim is a young middle-class industrialist from the provinces, Andrey Belugin, who has fallen in love with the impoverished aristocrat Elena Karmina, and for her sake adapts to the ways of Moscow society. Elena, in love with the equally impoverished young sophisticate Agishin, schemes to marry Belugin, so that Agishin and she can go abroad to lead a life of luxury on Belugin's money.

After a month of refusing Belugin his conjugal rights while accepting generous sums from him, Elena cannot keep up the deception. She asks Agishin to make their relationship clear by going away with her. Avoiding the issue, Agishin insists that they must first obtain still more money from Belugin.

Meanwhile Belugin, too, insists that his wife and her lover should remove themselves from his sight with as much money as she wishes. She learns that Belugin is himself leaving Moscow to work in his parents' factory. She can tell him that she has never consummated the affair with Agishin and now has come to love and respect him. So husband and wife depart happily for the provinces.

Again, as in *Easy Money*, a society belle has sought wealth through marriage to a successful businessman, who finally converts her to his industrious way of life. However, the contrast between the two life-styles is more acutely moral here, for the middle-class morality emerges as unambiguously admirable by comparison with the dishonest aristocratic concern for appearances and snobbish contempt for provincials. Elena's predecessor Lidia Cheboksarova is open in her feckless extravagance, and she does not deceive her husband from the start by pretending to love him as she conspires to make his best friend her lover. Morally worse than she, Elena finally experiences moral revulsion at her own deceit and her lover's cupidity, and converts to conjugal love and honesty.

Belugin represents the naive, honest, generous, innocent morality of the upper-middle class, a very different attitude from the scheming dishonesty of the lower-middle class which Ostrovsky castigated thirty years before in *A Family Affair*. True, Belugin is ridiculed for affecting high-society manners, wearing a tailcoat, bringing Elena bouquets and jewels, subjecting his provincial parents to scrutiny at her announcement party, and leading the life of the idle rich at balls and parties for a time with her. People mock him in society, as he ruefully admits to Elena. She, too, laughs at him after he has gone, even laughs at his proposal: "Ha, ha, ha! I shall be Mrs. Belugin, kitchen cook! Ha, ha, ha . . . rich, dressed to kill, with my Andrey Gavrilich at my side, in a luxury carriage with fine horses. . . . Ha, ha, ha . . . little Belugins!" (Act II, Sc. 2; VIII, 58–59). Her mother is shocked at her consenting to marry Belugin: "It isn't our sphere, my dear; their wild life, wild customs. . . . What will people say!" (Act II, Sc. 6; VIII, 65).

But Belugin turns out to be manly and admirable when, though still loving Elena, he sends her away with her lover. She admires him even more when before departure he dons the costume of his class: a long caftan, fur-trimmed and belted at the waist, and high boots. To be sure, he again lays himself open to ridicule when, explaining his change to a garb suited to crossing the factory yard to the laboratory, he distorts the learned word to "lobotory."

Still, as Elena learns from Tanya, Belugin's youthful sweetheart who has come to Moscow with her brother, life in the provincial city is by no means benighted. For instance, though the provincials seldom come to Moscow, they receive the latest fashions sooner than the metropolis by ordering direct from Paris.

Belugin does well to lack education in Agishin's sense, for to the latter education means adoption of the aristocrats's immoral code. Belugin is uneducated by reason of his high morals and nobility of heart, like Rousseau's noble savage. Agishin says of him: "He's in love, and how much in love! It isn't the same as with us! . . ." Nonaristocrats, he explains, fall in love "with their whole soul, that is with all their primal wildness!" (Act II, Sc. 5; VIII, 61). In Elena's mother, too, Agishin finds excessive cultivation of the higher feelings to be equivalent to a poor education. He gives the mother advice on overcoming an overemphasis on morality in her daughter's conduct: "[She must] give up idealistic principles, and take lightly certain duties and obligations" (Act III, Sc. 5; VIII, 76). Thus to the aristocrat education means orientation in a network of illicit relationships in which, however, appearances are preserved at all costs. Despite Leontev's warning against democratic opinions, Ostrovsky and Solovev have shown the aristocrats of the play to be self-seeking, cold, and dishonest.

Though Agishin parallels Telyatev in *Easy Money* by first sponsoring the outsider in society, he has no feeling for his friend. Nor in his aristocratic amoralism does he exhibit any devil-may-care charm like Telyatev's. He beats a coward's retreat when Belugin in ungentlemanly fashion tells him to leave at once if he doesn't want his legs broken.

In its plot structure the play conforms to the classic model. The fourth of its five acts even provides the requisite unexpected turn of events, a reversal in relations among all three major characters. With its final victory of simple business-class honesty over aristocratic double-dealing, this play has won the hearts of the proletarian nation: *The Marriage of Belugin* is among Ostrovsky's five most popular plays in the Soviet Union.

To be sure, its popularity may be partly due to its faults, among which the most notable is its lack of Ostrovskian ambiguity. Belugin is wholly admirable, and Agishin entirely contemptible. Elena is too naively noble for her role as seductress, unlike Kate Croy, the mistress in James's *Wings of the Dove*, who is hard and determined enough to be credible.

Is the coincidence of plot between this play and the novel of a quarter century later a case of actual communication between

Ostrovsky and James? The actress Maria Savina, who played Elena in the first St. Petersburg production of *The Marriage of Belugin* in January of 1878, might have served as a link between them, for she was close to Turgenev, with whom James became friendly just at this time. Or perhaps reality provided both writers independently with examples of a *ménage à trois* arrangement designed for making money and love concurrently.

CHAPTER 7

Ostrovsky Then and Now

I Ostrovsky Then

IN retrospect Ostrovsky's work of the second half of the nineteenth century represents a florescence of drama in Russia unparalleled in any Western European literature of the same period. Yet, though his work was recognized in his own country at the end of his life, recognition was freely given, on the whole, only by his contemporaries, the great novelists of the *Sovremennik* group—Goncharov, Turgenev, Tolstoy, and Grigorovich—and the great critics Chernyshevsky, Dobrolyubov, and Grigorev. After the all too early disappearance from public life of the critics who first welcomed his plays, Ostrovsky had to contend with hostile critics who kept repeating that he had "written himself out," or that he did not understand the postliberation era.

If critics of equal stature had arisen in the new era to elaborate the social significance of capitalism or the position of women as portrayed in Ostrovsky's plays, they might have emphasized not so much his unabated vitality as the continuity of theme from beginning to end of his career. For part of the disappointment with the later plays arose from the evolution of *samodurstvo* and "the dark kingdom" which Chernyshevsky and Dobrolyubov had identified in the early plays. Money and marriage, the themes of Ostrovsky's first work, continued to resound in the capitalist world of his later work, together with the new theme of an impoverished aristocracy. But Apollon Grigorev was no longer alive to proclaim all this "a new word in Russian literature."

After the liberation, the small businessmen of *A Family Affair* were becoming the big businessmen of *Easy Money, Wolves and Sheep,* and *Fiancée without Fortune.* The small world of Beyond-the-River Moscow has become a national scene with international implications. Though women and some men trained for no work still sell themselves in marriage, a few women choose the only work Ostrovsky sees as open to women, the acting profession. Ostrovsky's Realism of ordinary life hailed by the early critics still utilizes colloquial speech, though it is no longer the speech of Moscow. One of Ostrovsky's earlier critics, Dmitry Pisarev, who thought Dobrolyubov's attribution of political significance to *The Storm* exaggerated, and along with Apollon Grigorev saw in it a lyric reflection of folkways, is proved right: the lyric quality of Katherine in *The Storm* continues in Larisa of *Fiancée without Fortune,* and is reflected even in verse in *The Snow Maiden,* a progression to poetry which led Ostrovsky's politically minded editor, Nikolay Nekrasov, to reject the play.

Folkways are also reflected in faults of heroes and villains alike. The critics who were shocked that Lyubim Tortsov of *Poverty's No Vice* was a drunkard could have reacted in the same way to the drinking of Neschastlivtsev in *The Forest,* and of Matrena and Narkis in *A Warm Heart. Career Woman* shows an actress as no better than she should be.

The authority of the *samodurs* is no longer absolute after liberation; they become successively more ineffectual from Kabanikha through Gurmyzhskaya to Murzavetskaya. Yet the later figures are none the less memorable, just as a negative figure of another kind—the scoundrel Glumov—became an archetype outside the frame of Ostrovsky's play when Saltykov-Shchedrin incorporated him in his work. (See pp. 76.)

If the Realistic continuum of "the open ending" yields to the surprise ending of the late contrived plots, still no *raisonneur* recites a moral, or judges the characters at the final curtain. Are the manager types like Vasilkov in *Easy Money,* or Berkutov in *Wolves and Sheep,* to be viewed positively or negatively? Have Pribytkov in *The Final Sacrifice* and Velikatov in *Career Woman* acted as protectors or predators? Who is to blame for Xenia's death in *Not of This World:* her husband or she?

Though the relationships in the later plays are more complicated than the clear antitheses Dobrolyubov distinguished in the early work, villains are not wholly absent, and Ostrovsky's work is morally edifying implicitly, if not explicitly. His near villains, only some of whom are brought down, range from Podkhalyuzin of *A Family Affair,* through Vyshnevsky of *A Profitable Post* and the war lord in *Dream on the Volga,* to Murov in *Guilty without Guilt,* and the at least Mephisphelean Murugov in *Not of This World.* For Ostrovsky believed in the dramatist's high mission as promoter of culture and edification. This led Anatoly Lunacharsky, the first minister of culture after the October Revolution, to cite Ostrovsky's work as a model for the new Soviet drama he hoped would appear: "Molière, Goldoni and Ostrovsky," he wrote in 1923, "were remarkable in that, as representatives of a new class, they tried to hold up a mirror to their time," and "to teach while entertaining."[1]

II Ostrovsky Now

While Lunacharsky thus relaunched Ostrovsky in the twentieth century, Vladimir Mayakovsky tried to shut out the much younger Chekhov, who had continued many of the nineteenth-century playwright's traditions. In *Mystery-Bouffe*, a spectacle designed to show the Revolution in its entirety, Mayakovsky had this to say about drawing-room comedy:

> You look and see—
> Auntie Mames
> and Uncle Johnnies
> Sit talking through their noses on the couch.
> But we couldn't care less
> About aunties and uncles.
>   (11. 39–43, Prologue to *Mystery-Bouffe*, second variant)[2]

As a Futurist, Mayakovsky must logically scrap the past, as he does in the poem of 1923 from which our epigraph is taken, and in scorning Chekhov, of course he rejects Ostrovsky, who fathered Chekhov in many ways.

Indeed, the claim that Chekhov admired Ostrovsky is often made on the basis of a particular passage from a Chekhov letter of 1892 to Aleksey Suvorin "Yesterday [the actor Alexander] Lensky sent me a ticket to a performance by his pupils, who played [Ostrovsky's] *Slough of Despond* at the Maly. An astonishing play. The last act is something I would give a million to have written."[3] Surely such praise means that Lensky's pupils had worked a miracle with this sentimental piece.

Evidently Maria Savina's acting in the lead role did not do as much for *The Poor Bride* when Chekhov saw it, for he wrote of this fine early play to an actor friend in 1890: "The theaters here [in St. Petersburg] are unusually boring. I saw *The Poor Bride. . . .* The acting was typical of government-subsidized theater: uninspired and wooden."[4]

Chekhov had displayed an interest in Ostrovsky earlier than this. In 1888 he wrote the prolific journalist and fiction writer Nikolay Leykin: "If I were you, I would write a short novel on business-class life in the manner of Ostrovsky. I'd describe lawyers and devilish women; I'd take as subject monotonous, smooth, ordinary life as it, in fact, is, and I'd show business-class happiness. . . . The life of the Russian who buys and sells is very full, useful, sensible, and typical. . . ."[5] Clearly Chekhov admired Ostrovsky's depiction of what seems uneventful, everyday reality.

A year later in a letter to Suvorin Chekhov deplored the lack of comprehension which *The Storm* had encountered when it was performed in France in translation. Suvorin had published in his *Novoe vremya* the interview of a Paris correspondent with Ostrovsky's daughter in which it was explained that the French had seen *The Storm* as merely a romantic melodrama, without any social implications.

Chekhov's preference for Ostrovsky's portrayal of everyday life led him to reject the poetic fairy tale *The Snow Maiden*. Thus in 1900 he wrote his wife, the actress Olga Knipper, who had played a leading role in its production by the Moscow Art Theater: "Your theater should stage only contemporary plays, and nothing else! You ought to show contemporary life, as the intelligentsia lives it. . . ."[6]

In sum, as a beginning playwright Chekhov admired Ostrovsky's plays, though not as they were performed by the establishment theater. He saw them as for the most part contemporary, though, like his own, they would all too soon recede into the past of quaint customs and costumes, and he especially valued their social significance. He required the playwright to portray his own class, which Ostrovsky occasionally attempted by picturing theater people, though never by portraying writers, as Chekhov did in *The Sea Gull*. Neither portrayed the intelligentsia as such, though Chekhov's characters frequently act like members of the intelligentsia. Both pictured *raznochintsy*, or the classless who filled the ranks of the intelligentsia and ambitiously tried to rise in the mobile society of postliberation, capitalist Russia. The scoundrel Glumov and Vasilkov in *Easy Money* are such, as are Natasha in *The Three Sisters* and Lopakhin in *The Cherry Orchard*. The impoverished aristocrats Telyatev in *Easy Money* and Ranevskaya in *The Cherry Orchard* are both incapable of taking money seriously. Ostrovsky's

Negina in *Career Woman* and Chekhov's Nina in *The Sea Gull* are first and foremost actresses. Aunt Anfusa in *Wolves and Sheep* and Gaev in *The Cherry Orchard* are both ridiculously inarticulate; Glafira in *Wolves and Sheep* and Masha in *The Sea Gull* wear black, though for different reasons. Balzaminov's vulgar, simple-minded dreams of bliss belong in a humorous story by Chekhov.

More striking than common subject matter, however, are certain devices both playwrights used. Thus both *The Poor Bride* and *The Three Sisters* have "open endings," for the heroines must go on living despite their unhappiness. Another device is the use of happy background music contrasting with unhappy action: thus Larisa dies to gypsy music in *Fiancée without Fortune*, and the sisters learn of Tuzenbach's death while the band plays for the departing regiment. Both playwrights use allusive, or even "speaking," names.

The major trait common to Ostrovsky and Chekhov is at the same time a major difference between them. In discussing Chekhov, David Magarshack confusingly speaks of "plays of indirect action": "that is plays in which the main dramatic action takes place off-stage, and in which the action shown the audience on the stage is mainly 'inner action.' "[7] Indeed Chekhov does relegate important events, such as Treplev's suicide, to the wings, whereas Ostrovsky confronts us with them, as when he has Larisa die on stage. But "inner action" is often not made explicit in Ostrovsky either: an example is Larisa's change of heart when she sings the Baratynsky song against Karan-dyshev's wish. Lakshin even goes so far as to say: "By the poetry of what it does not make explicit *Fiancée without Fortune* surpasses the poetry of the Chekhovian play."[8] This may be exaggerated, but Lakshin is undoubtedly right in attributing "poetry" to such figures of Ostrovsky's as Katherine *(The Storm)* and Larisa. Chekhov's Nina and Treplev share that lyricism, at least in the first act of *The Sea Gull*.

Though Ostrovsky shows common traits with other later dramatists—for instance the anticlericalism which Maxim Gorky and he express through the hypocritically religious figures in their work—the nineteenth-century dramatist lives not by the heritage he has passed on to others, but by his own merits. In a tally of performances for the period from the playwright's death until 1917 Vladimir Filippov and N. Kashin show that Ostrovsky's plays of contemporary content were more often performed than his histori-cal plays, in part because the contemporary plays were simply less expensive to stage. Further, the plays written in collaboration have almost disappeared from the repertory, although *The Marriage of Belugin* had been very popular for a time.

Among Ostrovsky's contemporary plays those with starring roles for a great actress have been frequently performed. Following a temporary decline in the number of productions from Ostrovsky's death until the Revolution, after 1917 his plays were produced more frequently, with *The Forest* in first place and *Guilty without Guilt* in second. The increase which Filippov and Kashin note for the forty-odd years of their count has continued with a recent rise in the number of productions for the year 1973 honoring the one-hundred-fiftieth anniversary of Ostrovsky's birth.

On the whole, the operas based on Ostrovsky's plays—*Dream on the Volga* by Anton Arensky, *The Snow Maiden* by Nikolay Rimsky-Korsakov, and *Katya Kabanova* (after *The Storm*) by Leoš Janáček—are given only infrequently.

Quantity—that is, number of performances—may serve as an index of the interest Ostrovsky's work arouses in twentieth-century audiences. The quality of his work is confirmed by the directors and actors who have worked with his plays in the last half century, a list of whom amounts to a roster of the great in the performing arts of the time.

The first productions offered in response to Lunacharsky's slogan "Back to Ostrovsky" were done in the spirit of the 1920s, in the style of that decade's radical -isms. Should the series of acrobatic numbers into which Sergei Eisenstein and Sergey Tretyakov transformed *The Diary of a Scoundrel* in 1923 be called Dada or Futurism? Vsevolod Meyerhold produced *The Forest* with sets in height, and so in a style which could be called Constructivist. He too used gymnastics to dramatize the elan with which Aksyusha and Peter escape from authority to a new life of freedom, and he underscored their liberation with a song to accordion accompaniment, which then became a hit song of the day. Another avant-garde director, Alexander Tairov, produced *The Storm* in 1924 with the great actress Alicia Koonen as Katherine. Konstantin Stanislavsky's "stylized" production of *A Warm Heart* (1926) not only remained in the repertory of the Moscow Art Theater for a half century, but also struck the German playwright and director Bertolt Brecht as the most impressive production he saw in Moscow in the 1930s. Even now critics still argue over conceptions of a role, say Pribytkov's

(The Final Sacrifice) as acted by Vasily Merkuriev at the Pushkin Theater in Leningrad, or a negative view of the capitalist Vasilkov as seen from the Communist standpoint.

Is Ostrovsky better "contemporized," as in Meyerhold's *Forest*, or acted traditionally, as in the recent *Final Sacrifice* at the Pushkin Theater (directed, incidentally, by Meyerhold's daughter Irina)? Undoubtedly Ostrovsky deserves to be better known in the West today. For his major themes of money and marriage remain topical under modern Western capitalism, too, and his depiction of women has gained in relevance through the recent renewal of feminism. Although, on the one hand, possibilities for women today include more than marriage or the theater, on the other hand, capitalism in the West has changed less by comparison with the nineteenth century than has the Russian sociopolitical system under Soviet communism. The human problems, of course, remain the same, and Ostrovsky's gaze confronts them as unflinchingly, yet humanely, now as then. How could such heroes and heroines as Zhadov, Balzaminov, and Neschastlivtsev, or Katherine, Larisa, and Negina, fail to come alive in the West, if they were given their day on stage?

Notes and References

Epigraph

1. Vladimir Maiakovskii, *Polnoe sobranie sochinenii* v 13 tt. (Complete Collected Works in 13 vols.) (Moscow, 1955–61), V, 164, 11. 527–31:

> Go back
> to ivory,
> to the mammoth,
> back to
> Ostrovsky.

The lines taken from a 20-page ode of praise "To the workers of Kursk who mined the first ore" (1923) refer ironically to the revolutionary education minister Anatoly Lunacharsky's slogan "Back to Ostrovsky." (See also Preface and p. 134.)

Preface

1. L. N. Tolstoi, *Sobranie sochinenii* v 20 tt. (Collected Works in 20 vols.), ed. N. K. Gudzii et al. (Moscow, 1960–65), XVII, 150 (Letter 50 of January 29, 1857).
2. E. Kholodov, *Dramaturg na vse vremena* (A Dramatist for All Seasons) (Moscow, 1975), p. 48.

Chapter One

1. K. Shapiro, *Portretnaia galereia russkikh pisatelei*, vyp. I (A Portrait Gallery of Russian Writers, Issue I) (St. Petersburg, 1880); quoted in V. Lakshin, *Ostrovskii* (Moscow, 1976, pp. 29, 33–34 (cited below as Lakshin)).
2. Documents on Alexander's early life, registration of his birth, his petition for dismissal from the university, and two applications for his court job are attested by M. S. Ivanova, "Materialy dlia biografii Ostrovskogo" (Materials for a Biography of Ostrovsky) in *A. N. Ostrovskii, Literaturnoe nasledstvo* (A. N. Ostrovsky, Literary Heritage), v. 88, Pt. I (Moscow, 1974), pp. 449–54.
3. A. N. Ostrovskii, *Polnoe sobranie sochinenii* v 12 tt. (Complete Collected Works in 12 vols.) (Moscow, 1973–), I, 32 (cited below as PSS 12).
4. Quoted in Lakshin, p. 77.
5. See E. I. Prokhorov, "Ostrovskii i Gogol' " (Ostrovsky and Gogol), *Literaturnoe nasledstvo*, v. 88, Pt. I, pp. 439–48.

6. Quoted in Lakshin, p. 122.

7. Ibid., p. 123.

8. Ibid., p. 124.

9. A. N. Ostrovskii, PSS 12, XI, 30–31 (Letter 15).

10. PSS 12, XI, 57 (Letter 53).

11. Apollon Grigorev wrote thus in the first of four articles surveying Russian literature in 1851 (*Moskvitianin* [The Muscovite], Nos. 1–4, 1852). When challenged by Alexander Druzhinin in 1852 as to what that "new word" might be, Grigorev only repeated his slogan in the poem "Iskusstvo i pravda" (Art and Truth):

> The poet, prophet of a new truth,
> Surrounded us with a new world
> And said a new word,
> Though he served an old truth.

(Apollon Grigor'ev, *Izbrannye proizvedeniia* [Selected Works] [Moscow, 1959], p. 139: see also Note, p. 543.)

12. Ibid., p. 140.

13. Diaries in PSS 12, X, 350.

14. PSS 12, X, 358–59.

15. *Morskoi sbornik* (Marine Anthology), No. 2, 1859.

16. PSS 12, X, 463–522.

17. PSS 12, XI, 686 (Letter 806 of December 31, 1879).

18. Quoted in Lakshin, p. 360.

19. PSS 12, XI, 228 (Letter 235 of September 25, 1866).

20. After the first performance of *A Family Affair* in the uncensored version at the Pushkin Theater of Anna Brenko, Moscow, Ostrovsky was presented with a gold wreath.

21. Vladimir Kashperov, *The Storm* (1867); Peter Tschaikovsky, *Dream on the Volga* (1869); Nikolay Rimsky-Korsakov, *The Snow Maiden* (1882).

22. PSS 12, X, 91.

23. PSS 12, X, 462.

24. PSS 12, X, 147.

25. Ibid.

26. PSS 12, X, 148.

27. PSS 12, X, 147.

28. A. N. Ostrovskii, *Sobranie sochinenii v 10 tt.* (Collected Works in 10 vols.) (Moscow, 1959–60), X, 377.

29. PSS 12, X, 247.

Chapter Two

1. Apollon Grigor'ev, *Sochineniia* (Works), ed. V. Krupitch (Villanova, Pa., 1970), 48–49.

2. V. Ia. Lakshin, "Ostrovskii (1843–54)," in PSS 12, I, 477.

3. N. A. Dobroliubov, *Sobranie sochineniia* v 9 tt. (Collected Works in 9 vols.) (Leningrad, 1961–64), V, 30.

4. Norman Henley, "Ostrovskij's Play-Actors, Puppets and Rebels," *Slavic and East European Journal* 15 (1970): 317–25.

5. Dobrolyubov makes Masha's mother, as one who has herself been oppressed, therefore the instrument of Masha's oppression: ". . . she [the mother] had grown up . . . in such chains as to deprive her of any capacity for independent action. . . . Women generally who have been thus beaten down . . . in 'the dark kingdom' can themselves practice *samodurstvo* . . ." (Dobroliubov, V, 127).

6. A. A. Grigor'ev, *Sochineniia* (Works) (St. Petersburg, 1876), I, 59.

7. Ibid.

8. A. V. Druzhinin, *Sobranie sochinenii* (Collected Works) (St. Petersburg, 1865–67), VIII, 536–38.

9. For a brief survey of the broad spectrum of critical opinion upon the play's first appearance, see E. L. Efremenko's commentary to *Stay in Your Own Lane* in PSS 12, I, 544.

10. PSS 12, XI, 57 (Letter 53).

11. Ibid.

12. Dobroliubov, V, 72.

13. See Chapter I, p. 15, and Note 12.

14. F. M. Dostoevskii, *Pis'ma* v 4 tt. (Letters in 4 vols.) (Moscow, 1928–59), I, 306 (Letter 154 of August 24, 1861).

15. Ibid.

16. Quoted in E. I. Prokhorov, "Ostrovskii i Gogol'," *Literaturnoe nasledstvo*, v. 88, Pt. I, p. 440.

17. A. L. Shtein, *Master russkoi dramy* (A Master of Russian Drama) (Moscow, 1973), p. 106 (cited below as Shtein).

Chapter Three

1. Shtein, p. 207.

2. E. G. Kholodov, "A. N. Ostrovskii v 1855–65 gg." (A. N. Ostrovsky, 1855–65), in PSS 12, II, 666.

3. L. N. Tolstoi, *Sobranie sochinenii* v 20 tt. (Collected Works in 20 vols.) (Moscow, 1960–65), XVII, 150 (Letter 50 to V. P. Botkin of January 29, 1857).

4. From the periodical *Iakor'* (Anchor) 31 (1863); quoted in Prokhorov's commentary in PSS 12, II, 708.

5. N. G. Chernyshevskii, *Polnoe sobranie sochinenii* v 16 tt. (Complete Collected Works in 16 vols.) (Moscow, 1939–53), IV, 732.

6. See V. Ia. Lakshin, "Ob otnoshenii Ostrovskogo k Dobroliubovu" (On Ostrovsky's Relationship to Dobroliubov), *Voprosy literatury* (Questions of Literature) 2 (1959): 192–95.

7. D. I. Pisarev, *Sochineniia* v 4 tt. (Works in 4 vols.) (Moscow, 1955–56), II, 368, 377.

8. Iu. Osnos, *V mire dramy* (In the World of Drama) (Moscow, 1971), p. 221.

9. I. Goncharov, "Otzyv o drame 'Groza' " (Review of the Play *The Storm*) in *A. N. Ostrovskii v russkoi kritike* (A. N. Ostrovsky in Russian Criticism) (2nd ed., Moscow, 1953), p. 372.

10. Apollon Grigor'ev, *Literaturnaia kritika* (Moscow, 1967), p. 383.

11. Ibid., p. 384.

12. Ibid., p. 368.

13. Ibid., p. 410.

14. Pisarev, op. cit., II, 394.

15. Grigor'ev, op. cit., pp. 528–29.

16. Ibid., p. 419.

17. Quoted after Prokhorov's commentary in PSS 12, II, 777, from an unnamed critic in the journal *Illiustratsia* (Illustration) of January 31, 1863.

18. Grigor'ev, op. cit., p. 420.

19. Ibid., p. 419.

20. Ibid.

Chapter Four

1. L. Lotman, "Istoricheskaia dramaturgiia 60–80-x godov i tvorchestvo Ostrovskogo," *A. N. Ostrovskii i russkaia dramaturgiia ego vremeni* ("The Historical Plays of the 1860s to 1880s and Ostrovsky's Work," A. N. Ostrovsky and the Literature of the Theater in His Time) (Moscow, Leningrad, 1961), pp. 245–78.

2. Quoted in ibid., p. 246.

3. PSS 12, XI, 165 (Letter 163).

4. PSS 12, VI, 580.

5. See N. P. Kashin, *Etiudy ob Ostrovskom* (Studies on Ostrovsky) (Moscow, 1912), I, 203–35; also in A. N. Ostrovskii, *Dnevniki i pis'ma* (Diaries and Letters), ed. N. P. Kashin, "Academia" (Moscow, Leningrad, 1937), p. 205.

6. Wilhelm Tell to Parricida, nephew of the Austrian Emperor, who has just assassinated his sovereign and uncle because he felt his own right of succession has been jeopardized:

> I raise my clean hands to Heaven,
> Curse you and your deed . . .
> You have committed murder,
> While I have defended all I hold dear.
>
> (Act V, Sc. 2)

7. Shtein, p. 253.

Chapter Five

1. I. A. Goncharov, "Materialy zagotovliaemye dlia kriticheskoi stat'i ob Ostrovskom" (Materials for a Critical Article on Ostrovsky) in Goncharov, *Sobranie sochinenii v 8 tt.* (Collected Works in 8 vols.) (Moscow, 1952–55), VIII, 182.

2. The title of the adaptation by Rodney Ackland (London, 1948).

3. V. Lakshin, "Ostrovskii (1868–71)" in PSS 12, III, 476.

4. Quoted in Lakshin, PSS 12, III, 473.

5. See Lakshin's commentary in PSS 12, III, 508; from S. Dreiden, *V zritel'nom zale—Vladimir Il'ich* (In the Audience—Vladimir Il'ich [Lenin]) (Moscow, 1967), p. 178.

6. Quoted in Lakshin's commentary in PSS 12, III, 502, from an unnamed critic in the journal *Nedelia* (This Week) 49 (1868).

7. Quoted in Lakshin's commentary, PSS 12, III, 499, from the critic Neznakomets (A. S. Suvorin) in *Sanktpeterburgskie vedemosti* (St. Petersburg Gazette) for November 3, 1868.

8. Lakshin, op. cit., Note 3 above, PSS 12, III, 484.

9. S. S. Danilov and M. G. Portugalova, *Russkii dramaticheskii teatr XIX veka* (The Russian Dramatic Theater of the Nineteenth Century) (Leningrad, 1974), II, 71.

10. PSS 12, III, 483.

11. Rather, one of the characters in *Teatral'nyi raz'ezd posle predstavleniia novoi komedii* (Dispersal of the Audience after the Performance of a New Comedy) asks one of the actors: "How can one give an audience pleasure by playing the part of a rascal?" N. V. Gogol', *Polnoe sobranie sochinenii v 14 tt.* (Complete Collected Works in 14 vols.) (Moscow, 1937–52), IV, 123. The very real fact of such a possibility gives rise to the professional theater 'concept of "an actor of negative fascination" (see Shtein, p. 194).

12. Quoted in L. N. Smirnova's commentary in PSS 12, III, 523, from the journal *Delo* (The Cause) 11 (1871).

13. Quoted in Smirnova's commentary in PSS 12, III, 524, from *Zaria* (Dawn) 3 (1870).

14. Quoted in Smirnova's commentary in PSS 12, III, 525, from *Otechestvennye zapiski* (Fatherland Notes) 1, 2 (1875).

15. Quoted in Smirnova's commentary in PSS 12, III, 524, from *Novoe vremia* (New Time), April 22, 1870.

16. "Das Ideal und das Leben," a poem by Friedrich Schiller.

17. Mary McCarthy, "Nicolo Chiarmonte and the Theatre," *New York Review of Books* 22:2 (February 20, 1975):28.

18. PSS 12, XI, 470 (Letter 541).

19. PSS 12, XI, 441 (Letter 499).

20. PSS 12, X, 233.

21. Ibid.

22. Goncharov, *Sobranie sochinenii* v 8 tt., VIII, 170.

23. Quoted in Z. A. Bliumina's commentary, PSS 12, IV, 497–98, from *Russkaia mysl'* (Russian Thought) 9 (1900).

Chapter Six

1. PSS 12, XI, 571 (Letter 671 of October 29, 1877).

2. V. E. Meyerhold, *Stat'i. Pis'ma. Rechi. Besedy* (Articles. Letters. Speeches. Talks), 2 vols. (Moscow, 1968), II, 265.

3. *A. N. Ostrovskii i F. A. Burdin* (A. N. Ostrovsky and F. A. Burdin) (Moscow, Petrograd, 1923), p. 235.

4. PSS 12, XI, 578–79 (Letter 678 of November 16, 1877).

5. See Smirnova's commentary in PSS 12, IV, 539.

6. Though, like Kalinov, Bryakhimov no longer exists today, it was in ancient times located near the modern Vasilsursk on the upper reaches of the Volga, as E. I. Prokhorova informs in her commentary, PSS 12, V, 504.

7. See PSS 12, XI, 662 Letter 780 of October 11, 1879, for a similar idea.

8. Iurii M. Iur'ev, *Zapiski* (Notes) (Leningrad, Moscow, 1963), II, 35.

9. Ibid., p. 34.

10. Two renderings of Ostrovsky's play—Iakov Protazanov's cinematic version of 1937, and a Moscow Art Theater production of the 1950s—had Larisa shot in the back by Karandyshev as she left to go to Knurov. But this contradicts the stage directions: "Karandyshev comes up to the table and sits down opposite Larisa" (Act IV, Sc. 10; PSS 12, V, 79), and then "Karandyshev (shoots her with his pistol). Larisa (seizing her chest): Oh! I thank you! (Sinks down on a chair)" (Act IV, Sc. 11; PSS 12, V, 81). Unmistakably, then, Larisa was facing her fiancé and had by no means turned to go.

11. Quoted after Prokhorov's commentary in PSS 12, V, 519, from Ostrovsky's conversation with the actors M. I. Pisarev and P. A. Strepetova; see also V. Lakshin, "Novye materialy ob A. N. Ostrovskom" (New Materials on A. N. Ostrovsky), *Russkaia literatura* (Russian Literature) 1 (1960):154.

12. Quoted in Prokhorov's commentary in PSS 12, V, 520, from *Novoe vremia*, January 16, 1882.

13. Ibid., December 25, 1881.

14. Iur'ev, *Zapiski*, I, 212.

15. V. Lakshin, "Ostrovskii (1878–86)," in PSS 12, V, 494.

16. PSS 12, V, 493.

17. E. Kholodov, *Dramaturg na vse vremena*, p. 136.

18. N. S. Grodskaia, "Iz tvorcheskoi istorii p'esy 'Bez viny vinovatye' " (On the History of the Composition of *Guilty without Guilt*), *Literaturnoe nasledstvo*, v. 88, Pt. I, pp. 511–31.

19. Lakshin, PSS 12, V, 495.

20. P. Markov, " 'Bez viny vinovatye' " (*Guilty without Guilt*), in *A. N. Ostrovskii na sovietskoi stsene* (A. N. Ostrovsky on Soviet Stages) (Moscow, 1974), pp. 90–91.

21. Grodskaia, p. 531.

22. The subtitle "Family Scenes" of this, Ostrovsky's last play, recalls the title of his first, "A Family Scene" (Semeinaia kartina) (1846): see PSS 12, I, 499.

23. Quoted in Prokhorov's commentary in PSS 12, V, 540, from *Moskovskie vedomosti* (Moscow Gazette), January 10, 1885. Flerov (pseudonym of Sergei Vasil'ev) wrote not only a longer article on this play, but also the survey article "A. N. Ostrovskii i nash teatr" (A. N. Ostrovsky and Our Theater), *Russkoe obozrenie* (Russian Survey) 4:6 (1890).

24. Quoted in E. N. Dunaeva, "Ostrovskii v perepiski N. Ia. Solov'eva i K. N. Leont'eva" (Ostrovsky in the Correspondence between N. Ia. Solovev and K. N. Leontev), *Literaturnoe nasledstvo*, v. 88, Pt. I, p. 568.

25. See Dunaeva and also L. Danilova's commentary in PSS 12, VIII, 399–405.

26. Ostrovsky's wife is the target of barbs directed against her by the actor in a letter to Solovev dating from the last year of the collaboration, in which Sadovsky writes: "I am heartily glad that your work is finished; I'd be curious to know one thing: did you manage to get rid of Alexander Nikolaevich [Ostrovsky]'s collaboration or not?" L. R. Lanskii, "Ostrovskii v neizdannoi perepiske sovremennikov" (Ostrovsky in the Previously Unpublished Correspondence of his Contemporaries), *Literaturnoe nasledstvo*, v. 88, Pt. I, p. 615 (Letter of August 28, 1880).

Chapter Seven

1. A. V. Lunacharskii, "A. N. Ostrovskii i po povodu ego" (A. N. Ostrovsky and Concerning Him), *O teatre i dramaturgii* (On the Theater and the Literature of the Theater), 2 vols. (Moscow, 1958), I, 239.

2. Vladimir Maiakovskii, *Polnoe sobranie sochinenii v 13 tt.* (Complete Collected Works in 13 vols.) (Moscow, 1955–61), II, 248. Mayakovsky's ridicule of *The Three Sisters*, as if he had seen it all too often, is implicit in the familiarity of "Mame" for Masha, and a plurality of Johnnies for Uncle Vanya.

3. A. P. Chekhov, *Polnoe sobranie sochinenii i pisem v 20 tt.* (Complete Collected Works and Letters in 20 vols.) (Moscow, 1944–51), XV, 332–33 (Letter of March 3, 1892).

4. Ibid., XV, 12 (Letter of January 28, 1890 to Alexander Sumbatov-Iuzhin).

5. Ibid., XIV, 110 (Letter of May 11, 1888).

6. Ibid., XVIII, 400 (Letter of September 28, 1900).

7. David Magarshack, *Chekhov the Dramatist* (New York, 1960), p. 53.

8. PSS 12, V, 481.

Selected Bibliography

PRIMARY SOURCES

1. In Russian

Sobranie sochinenii v 10 tt. (Collected Works in 10 vols.). Vols. 1–8, St. Petersburg: A. A. Kraevskii, 1874. Vol. 9, Moscow: F. I. Salaev, 1878. Vol. 10, St. Petersburg: E. I. Kekhribardzhi, 1884.

Polnoe sobranie sochinenii v 12 tt. (Complete Collected Works in 12 vols.). Ed. Modest Ivanovich Pisarev. St. Petersburg: Prosveshchenie, 1904–1905.

Polnoe sobranie sochinenii v 16 tt. (Complete Collected Works in 16 vols.). Ed. A. I. Reviakin, G. I. Vladykin, V. A. Filippov. Moscow: Gosudarstvennoe izdatel'stvo khydozhestvennoi literatury, 1949–53.

Stikhotvornye dramy (Verse Plays). Ed. and introd. by Lidiia Mikhailovna Lotman. Second edition. Leningrad: Sovetskii pisatel' (Biblioteka poeta, Bol'shaia seriia), 1961.

Polnoe sobranie sochinenii v 12 tt. (Complete Collected Works in 12 vols.). Ed. G. I. Vladykin, I. V. Il'inskii, V. Ia. Lakshin, V. I. Malikov, P. A. Markov, A. D. Salynskii, E. G. Kholodov. Moscow: Iskusstvo, 1973–. (In press: Latest volume, vol. 11, *Pis'ma* (1848–80). Ed. V. Lakshin. Moscow, 1979.)

2. Translations of Ostrovsky's Plays into English

Note: the English titles used in this study for Ostrovsky's plays are listed alphabetically. Only those translations are so listed which are still available according to *Books in Print 1977–78.*

Career Woman [Talanty i poklonniki]. *Artistes and Admirers.* Tr. Elisabeth Hanson. Manchester: Manchester Univ. Press; New York: Barnes & Noble, 1976.

The Diary of a Scoundrel [Na vsiakogo mudretsa dovol'no prostoty]. *The Scoundrel.* Tr. Eugene K. Bristow, in Eugene K. Bristow. Tr. & ed. *Five Plays of Alexander Ostrovsky.* New York: Pegasus, 1969, pp. 277–356. *Even A Wise Man Stumbles.* Tr. David Magarshack, in David Magarshack. *Easy Money and Two Other Plays.* Westport, Conn.: Greenwood Press, 1970 (reprint of 1944 edition), pp. 13–93. *Even the Wise Can Err.* Tr. Margaret Wettlin, in Margaret Wettlin, *Alexander Ostrovsky, Plays.* Moscow: Progress Publishers, 1974, pp. 252–367.

Easy Money [Beshennye den'gi]. *Easy Money.* Tr. David Magarshack, in
Eric Bentley, ed. *From the Modern Repertoire,* Series 2. Bloomington:
Indiana Univ. Press, 1964 (reprint of 1952 edition), pp. 43–106. *Easy
Money and Two Other Plays.* Tr. David Magarshack. Westport, Conn.:

A Family Affair [Svoi liudi—sochtemsia!]. *It's a Family Affair—We'll Settle
It Ourselves.* Tr. Eugene K. Bristow, in Bristow. *Five Plays of Alexander Ostrovsky,* pp. 29–108. *It's a Family Affair—We'll Settle It Ourselves.* Tr. George Rapall Noyes, in George Rapall Noyes, ed. *Plays by
Alexander Ostrovsky.* New York: AMS Press Inc., 1969 (reprint of 1917
edition), pp. 215–305.

The Forest [Les]. *The Forest.* Tr. Eugene K. Bristow, in Bristow. *Five Plays
of Alexander Ostrovsky,* pp. 357–459.

Guilty without Guilt [Bez viny vinovatye]. *More Sinned against Than
Sinning.* Tr. Margaret Wettlin, in Wettlin. *Alexander Ostrovsky,
Plays,* pp. 368–473.

A Poor Bride [Bednaia nevesta]. *The Poor Bride.* Tr. Eugene K. Bristow, in
Bristow. *Five Plays of Alexander Ostrovsky,* pp. 109–203.

Poverty's No Vice [Bednost' ne porok]. *Poverty Is No Crime.* Tr. George
Rapall Noyes, in Noyes. *Plays by Alexander Ostrovsky,* pp. 67–133.

Sin and Sorrow Are Common to All [Grekh da beda na kogo ne zhivet]. *Sin
and Sorrow Are Common to All.* Tr. George Rapall Noyes, in Noyes.
Plays by Alexander Ostrovsky, pp. 137–212.

The Storm [Groza]. *The Storm.* Tr. Eugene K. Bristow, in Bristow. *Five
Plays of Alexander Ostrovsky,* pp. 203–76. *The Thunderstorm.* Tr.
George Rapall Noyes, in Barrett Harper Clark, ed. *World Drama,* v. 2.
New York: Dover Publications, 1956, pp. 608–41. *The Thunderstorm.*
Tr. Andrew MacAndrew, in John Gassner, ed. *A Treasury of the
Theatre,* v. 1. New York: Simon & Schuster, 1967, pp. 988–1012. *The
Storm.* Tr. David Magarshack, in David Magarshack, ed. *The Storm
and Other Russian Plays.* New York: Hill & Wang (Mermaid
Dramabook, MD 18), 1960, pp. 85–153. *The Storm.* Tr. Franklin D.
Reeve, in Franklin D. Reeve, ed. *Nineteenth Century Russian Plays.*
New York: W. W. Norton, 1973, pp. 315–74. *The Storm.* Tr. Margaret
Wettlin, in Wettlin. *Alexander Ostrovsky, Plays,* pp. 158–251.

The Ward [Vospitannitsa]. *A Protégée of the Mistress.* Tr. George Rapall
Noyes, in *Plays by Alexander Ostrovsky,* pp. 11–63.

Wolves and Sheep [Volki i ovtsy]. *Wolves and Sheep.* Tr. David Magarshack, in Magarshack. *Easy Money and Two Other Plays,* pp. 187–289.

SECONDARY SOURCES

1. Selected List
Note: all of the editions of Ostrovsky's works listed above contain critical
material on him, especially the most recent edition in twelve volumes, of
which almost every volume includes an essay by a scholar on the period

covered in the volume. The volumes of plays in translation here listed also contain introductions by their editors or translators to the plays they include.

ALPERS, BORIS VLADIMIROVICH. " 'Serdtse ne kamen' ' i pozdnii Ostrovskii," in Alpers, *Teatral 'nye ocherki* (Theater Essays), two vols. Moscow: Iskusstvo, 1977, I, 405–546. The critic Alpers's analyses of late plays as produced on stage, proving the variety of the work, and refuting the superficial view of it as conforming to a single stereotype.

A. N. Ostrovskii i literaturnoe teatral'noe dvizhenie XIX–XX vekov (A. N. Ostrovsky and the Literary Movement in the Theater of the Nineteenth and Twentieth Centuries). Ed. N. I. Prutskov. Leningrad: Nauka, 1974. An anthology of articles on Ostrovsky by such scholars as Danilova, Lotman, Lakshin, and Kholodov, writing on interesting subjects, for example, "Ostrovsky and modernism."

A. N. Ostrovskii na sovetskoi stsene: Stat'i o spetakliakh moskovskikh teatrov raznykh let (A. N. Ostrovsky on the Soviet Stage: Articles on Productions of Various Years in Moscow Theaters). Ed. T. N. Pavlova, E. G. Kholodov. Moscow: Iskusstvo, 1974. An illustrated collection of reviews by various critics on Moscow productions of plays by Ostrovsky from Sergei Eisenstein's *Diary of a Scoundrel* (1923) to L. V. Varpakhovsky's *Easy Money*, with Lunacharsky's article launching the slogan "Back to Ostrovsky" as a foreword and Kholodov's conclusion "Onward with Ostrovsky" as an afterword.

A. N. Ostrovskii: novye materialy i issledovaniia (A. N. Ostrovsky: New Materials and Research). *Literaturnoe nasledstvo*, v. 88 in two vols. Moscow: Nauka, 1974. In the first volume previously unpublished materials, largely letters pertaining to biography, or to certain plays, or to the reception of certain plays, and further, in the second volume articles on Ostrovsky's relations to theaters and actors. Also an article on Ostrovsky's reception in each of a dozen countries, including "Ostrovsky in the U.S." Finally, articles on miscellaneous topics, such as the Ostrovsky materials at Shchelykovo, the whole with interesting illustrations of good quality.

A. N. Ostrovskii v russkoi kritike (A. N. Ostrovsky in Russian Criticism). Ed. G. I. Vladykin. Moscow: Gosudarstvennoe izdatel'stvo khudozhestvennoi literatury, 1953. An anthology of the basic articles on Ostrovsky by the great critics except for Grigorev: two each by Chernyshevsky and Dobrolyubov, three by Goncharov, and one each by Lunacharsky, Dmitry Pisarev, Plekhanov, and Turgenev.

A. N. Ostrovskii v vospominaniiakh sovremennikov (A. N. Ostrovsky in the Recollections of His Contemporaries). Ed. A. I. Reviakin. Moscow: Gosudarstvennoe izdatel'stvo khudozhestvennoi literatury, 1966. Many brief recollections of the playwright. Especially notable among them are those by Ostrovsky's lifelong friend Burdin, and by actors Alexander Nil'skii and Maria Savina.

Bibliografiia literatury ob A. N. Ostrovskom (1847–1917) (Bibliography of Material on A. N. Ostrovsky, 1847–1917). Ed. K. D. Muratova. Leningrad: Nauka, 1974. A bibliography of just over six thousand items, books, and articles in journals and newspapers, with four alphabetical indices: Ostrovsky's works, theaters and institutions, names of persons, and names of newspapers and journals.

Biblioteka A. N. Ostrovskogo (A. N. Ostrovsky's Library). Ed. A. N. Stepanov. Leningrad: BAN SSSR, 1963. A catalogue of Ostrovsky's two libraries, one in Moscow, and one in Shchelykovo.

CHERNYSHEVSKII, NIKOLAI G. *Polnoe sobranie sochinenii* v 16 tt. (Complete Collected Works in 16 vols.) (1939–53), v. 2, "Stat'i i retsenzii (1853–55)" (Articles and Reviews, 1853–55). Ed. M. M. Grigor'ian. Moscow: Gosudarstvennoe izdatel'stvo khudozhestvennoi literatury, 1949, pp. 232–40. Reviews of *A Poor Bride* and *Poverty's No Vice*.

DOBROLIUBOV, NIKOLAI A. *Russkie klassiki* (Russian Classics). Ed. Iu. G. Oksman. Moscow: Nauka, 1970, pp. 70–188, 231–300. The two decisive articles "Temnoe tsarstvo" (1859), and "Luch sveta v temnom tsarstve" (1860) in the scholarly edition "Literaturnye pamiatniki."

EISOLD, WOLFGANG *Die Namen im Werk des Dramatikers A. N. Ostrovskij* (The Names in the Work of the Dramatist A. N. Ostrovsky). Dissertation der Freien Universität Berlin. Berlin, 1961. The "speaking" and allusive names in Ostrovsky's plays.

GRIGOR'EV, APOLLON. *Literaturnaia kritika* (Literary Criticism). Ed. B. F. Egorov. Moscow: Khudozhestvennaia literatura, 1967, pp. 367–404. The basic article, "Posle 'Grozy' Ostrovskogo: Pis'ma k I. S. Turgenevu," (After Ostrovsky's "Storm": Letters to I. S. Turgenev) in which the early work of Ostrovsky is seen as revealing the beauty, the feeling, and the language of the whole Russian people with a verity in some ways superior to Gogol's Realism.

KHOLODOV, EFIM GRIGOR'EVICH. *Dramaturg na vse vremena* (A Dramatist for All Seasons). Moscow: Vserossiiskoe teatral'noe obshchestvo, 1975. A comprehensive and perceptive survey of the reception of Ostrovsky's work seen both quantitatively and qualitatively in his own time and thereafter up to the present, including number of performances and criticism of interpretation in productions of the most popular plays.

———. *Masterstvo Ostrovskogo* (The Achievement of Ostrovsky). Second edition, Moscow: Iskusstvo, 1967. An illuminating study of form in Ostrovsky's work, its distinctive qualities, such as language, and its devices, e.g. "speaking names."

KOGAN, L. P. *Letopis' zhizni i tvorchestva A. N. Ostrovskogo* (Chronology of the Life and Work of A. N. Ostrovsky). Moscow: Kul'turno-prosvetitel'naia literatura, 1953. Chronology of Ostrovsky's life.

LAKSHIN, VLADIMIR IAKOVLEVICH. *Ostrovskii.* Moscow: Iskusstvo (Seriia "Zhizn' v iskusstve"), 1976. A readable and popularly written biography without scholarly apparatus in conformity with the series in which it appears. New material, more about the life than the work, with interesting illustrations of poor quality.

LOTMAN, LIDIIA MIKHAILOVNA. A. N. *Ostrovskii i russkaia dramaturgiia ego vremeni* (A. N. Ostrovsky and the Russian Dramatic Literature of His Time). Moscow, Leningrad: Akademiia nauk, 1961. The basic earlier treatise from the Soviet viewpoint by an eminent scholar, relating Ostrovsky to his literary predecessors, contemporaries, and successors.

————. Introductory article in Ostrovskii, *Stikhotvornye dramy*. (Biblioteka poeta), see this title under Primary Sources above: pp. 5–57.

Nasledie Ostrovskogo i sovetskaia kul'tura (The Ostrovsky Heritage and Soviet Culture). Ed. A. N. Reviakin. Moscow: Nauka, 1974. Twenty-four articles by less well-known specialists, some on "Ostrovsky and Russian Literature," (for example one on "Ostrovsky's Work as Evaluated by Apollon Grigor'ev,"); others on "Ostrovsky and the Theater" (for example an article on "Ostrovsky, the Director.")

PISAREV, DMITRII I. *Sochineniia* v 4 tt. (Works in 4 vols.), v. 2: "Motivy russkoi dramy" (Themes of Russian Drama). Moscow: 1955–56, pp. 366–95. Pisarev's argument against conscious protest on the part of Katherine in *The Storm*.

REVIAKIN, ALEKSANDR IVANOVICH. *Iskusstvo dramaturgii A. N. Ostrovskogo* (The Art of the Playwright A. N. Ostrovsky). Second edition, Moscow: Prosveshchenie, 1974. Helpful criticism of the plays in their chronological order with few but interesting illustrations of poor quality.

SHTEIN, ABRAM L'VOVICH. *Master russkoi dramy* (A Master of Russian Drama). Moscow: Sovetskii pisatel', 1973. Thoughtful and interesting single essays on the important plays from *A Family Affair* to *Fiancée without Fortune*, and a final assessment of Ostrovsky's place in literature.

2. Secondary Works in English

COX, LUCY. "Form and Meaning in the Plays of Alexander N. Ostrovsky." Diss. University of Pennsylvania 1975. Cox argues that ". . . while the earlier plays up to 1861 do indeed focus on the *byt* [the ordinary features of everyday life], later plays focus on character traits. . . . In the 'dramatic' [later] plays . . . incidents which create suspense . . . predominate over 'expositional' incidents. . . . [In *Wolves and Sheep*] the characters represent universal 'humors.' " *Dissertation Abstracts International* 36 (November 1975): 2887A–88A (cited hereafter as *DAI*).

GRYLACK, BEVIN RATNER. "The Function of Proverbs in the Dramatic Works of A. N. Ostrovsky." Diss. New York University 1975. *DAI* 36

(December 1975): 3906A–3907A. Not the proverbs used in fourteen titles and twelve subtitles of the forty-one plays Ostrovsky wrote between 1847 and 1855 are indicative of the frequency of proverbs occurring in the plays, which ranges from fifteen to fifty, but the speech characteristics and dramatic types reflected in them. Used by characters of two types, the philosopher Elokhov, *Not of This World*), and the matchmaker (Krasavina, the Balzaminov Trilogy), the proverbs lend the plays the new dimension of aphoristic generalization.

HENLEY, NORMAN. "Ostrovsky's Play-Actors, Puppets and Rebels." *Slavic and East European Journal,* 14 (1970): 317–25. Henley's title refers to three categories of characters he distinguishes in Ostrovsky's plays. He subdivides the first category of play-actors further into three sub-categories of self-seekers (Podkhalyuzin), *samodurs* (Bolshov), and the histrionically obsessed (Lyubim Tortsov). He defines the second category of puppets as all minor characters, the male lovers (Boris), and victims (Lynyaev, Larisa, and Negina—*sic!*). He classes as rebels Masha, Zhadov and Katherine. His classifications serve little purpose.

KASPIN, ALBERT. "Character and Conflict in Ostrovsky's *Talents and Admirers.*" *Slavic ad East European Journal* 8 (1964): 26–36. Calling the plot of this unusual play "commonplace enough," Kaspin, another classifier, divides the characters into those espousing the practical and those striving for the ideal in life—in other words, the wolves and the sheep. He sees Meluzov as "the moral victor" in the end, and takes an interesting but surely erroneous view of Bakin as Velikatov's accomplice.

———. "Dostoevsky's Masloboyev and Ostrovsky's Dosuzhev." *American Slavic and East European Review* 39 (1960): 222–26. Kaspin devotes only a couple of pages to Dosuzhev, placing him in Ostrovsky's work, and barely touching on the interesting topic of the relationship between Dostoevsky and Ostrovsky.

———. "A Re-Examination of Ostrovsky's Character Lyubim Tortsov." *Studies in Russian and Polish Literature,* No. 27. *In Honor of Waclaw Lednicki.* Ed. Zbigniew Folejewski. The Hague: Mouton, 1962, pp. 185–91. Kaspin's characterization of Lyubim is generally illuminating, though marred by words of infrequent usage in American, like "merry-andrew" and "tatter-demalion." Again he only touches on the potentially interesting subject of the link to Dostoevsky, though admitting that it is premature to tie it to this early period.

———. "A Superfluous Man and an Underground Man in Ostrovskij's *The Poor Bride.*" *Slavic and East European Journal* 6 (1962): 312–21. Khorkov, who is not of noble birth, has crossed class lines by graduating from the university, and so become a "superfluous man." The German idealistic philosophy he has learned has made him further unfit for the workaday world. However apt the case for calling Khorkov "superfluous" may be, the argument for Milashin as an "underground man" is less persuasive. Still, this article illuminates Ostrovsky's place in his time.

WETTLIN, MARGARET. "Alexander Ostrovsky and the Russian Theatre before Stanislavsky," in Wettlin. *Alexander Ostrovsky, Plays*, pp. 7–79. A readable biographical sketch of Ostrovsky, which becomes in midstream a discussion of actors in the theater of his time.

Index

WORKS: PLAYS

WORKS: PROSE